Parenting Love

Clever Ideas Learned
from Raising 200 Children

Kathleen Paydo, RN
With foreword by Ron Paydo

Kathleen M. Paydo, LLC
Wadsworth, Ohio, USA
KathleenPaydo.com

Editor: Susan Ciancio
Cover Design: Lynde R. Kosko

PARENTING LOVE

Kathleen Paydo RN – 1st edition

ISBN: 9798986474175

To all the children who came through our home,
know that you are in our hearts forever.

ACKNOWLEDGMENTS

I would like to express my gratitude to my dear family: to Ron, for continuing to always say yes; to Matthew, for being my communication consultant; to Elizabeth, for being my ever-patient proofreader and first line editor; to Katherine, for being my professional advisor and sounding board; to Melissa, for being my amazing publisher; and to Conner, for being my media and videography guru. You are the best teammates!

CONTENTS

FOREWORD

Parenting has never been a one-size-fits-all approach. Ask any parent and they will tell you that what worked for one child may not have worked for the next. And today, many of us are parenting in merged families of different shapes and sizes. In addition, teachers, coaches, and daycare staff "parent" our children as well. Whether we are raising our own or someone else's children, all children need love through boundaries and guidance.

Parenting Love: Clever Ideas Learned from Raising 200 Children offers tips and true-life experiences that through years of trial and error have worked well for my wife Kathleen, my family, and me. The reason we can cite so many firsthand examples is because Kathleen and I, who do have four biological children, also have been foster parents to over 200 children. We sit in the unique position of parenting many children in our home, so we see which parenting ideas work and which do not. Having lived with hundreds of children of all ages, from different backgrounds, and with varying temperaments, we now have an abundance of real-life experiences to share. Our parenting approach has evolved throughout the years because the unique personalities of each child and the circumstances that surround them have molded us into the parents we are today.

At the end of the day, we are doing the best we can to raise each child we encounter so they grow into strong and competent adults. No deep neuroscience here. This is more of a boots-on-the-ground experience that Kathleen and I want to share with all parents and parent figures. We are excited to take you on this journey with us!

Ron

PREFACE: A SHOE IN THE SINK

As a registered nurse, I learned many facts about the growth and development of a child, but the *art* of learning to parent effectively has evolved over time. Knowing that parenting beliefs are a multigenerational mindset, Ron and I, as veteran parents, want to teach excellent parenting skills to as many people as we are able.

Drawing from our experience, sifting through parenting books, and attending extensive training has led to the development of the ideas in this book. In our journey of parenting so many children, we have shed tears of both frustration and joy. I wrote this book in hopes of preventing some of the same challenges and offering learned insights to my readers. The ideas expressed here can translate well to any family looking for clever ideas to promote good behaviors in children.

Unconventional parenting ideas are meant to help us parents work smarter not harder. The shoe in the sink idea found itself into our home quite by accident but works like a charm when it comes to remembering the out-of-the-ordinary things that must be done. For instance, the tooth fairy has visited our house hundreds of times throughout the years. One day, our foster son Tre told me that he lost his tooth. I had also just accepted another sibling group of three that evening, so my head was in a hundred different places, and I knew that I would likely forget about his tooth fairy visit. As I walked up the steps, I needed something to jog my fatigued mind once baths and bedtime were done, so I grabbed the closest thing to me, which was a shoe. As I passed my bathroom, I dropped the shoe in my sink knowing I would see it before bed and remember why it was there. This worked like a charm, and when the children settled into bed for the night, I remembered my important task.

I have used this tactic and many others like it ever since because they remind me of the task without letting the children in on what I'm doing. Ron will even help remind me if he sees that the lone shoe is still around in the morning. (Regarding the tooth fairy, I also stash a few one-dollar bills in my room so I am always prepared for that delighted child who pulls a tooth out right before bedtime.) We quickly realized that this silly technique was a great way for us to silently signal each other to remember important details amongst the busyness of our household.

Useful ideas that work are worth passing along. Finding shortcuts, trying mnemonic assists, and highlighting unique techniques are the foundation of *Parenting Love: Clever Ideas Learned from Raising 200 Children*. These real-life experiences, expressed in stories, come from over thirty-five years of parenting. Our quest is to change the world for the better, one child at a time. So, listen to others' ideas, sort the good from the bad, and adopt what works for your family.

CHAPTER 1: A NEW MINDSET

Every child has a different story and varying experiences that make up who they are. Avoiding a streamlined one-size-fits-all approach and understanding the child's history as well as their point of view will help us know which parenting techniques will offer the best results.

UNDERSTANDING THEIR PAST

Behaviors are affected by how children perceive their world around them and why they respond the way they do. This in turn has everything to do with how they might best be parented. A good parenting mantra should be to support a child through their struggles but not to solve all their problems for them. When overcoming struggles happens on a small scale in childhood, we have a better chance of raising capable children who will be able to withstand bigger challenges in adulthood.

It's unorthodox but of paramount importance to know that good parenting advice starts with understanding childhood stress and trauma. While it can be distressing to think about a child's upbringing in this way, it's true that many children have experienced stress and trauma on some level. Stress can be mild, but trauma can range from complex to severe.

Many children have experienced some kind of significant stress or trauma during childhood. The degree of severity is often described in the parenting world through a term called ACEs or "adverse childhood experiences." According to the CDC, ACEs are "potentially traumatic events that occur in childhood" and include instability in the home and community, violence, abuse or neglect, family member death or suicide, or substance abuse problems.[1] The higher degree of ACEs involved, the more the likelihood of seeing children with behavioral difficulties.

An example of an ACE that might not result in trauma per se could be the lack of clean drinking water and healthy food, an absence of medical care, or how a divorce in the family is handled. Children can recover quickly if these basic needs are met by skillfully correcting the ailment and wrapping support around the child medically.

Children can come through divorce in good shape if the parents are amicable and the children are not pulled back and forth emotionally or asked to choose sides. Divorce can be done well, so even though this is likely a loss on some level, it might be considered more of a stress or mild trauma. One thought to keep the trauma low in a divorce scenario is to keep the blame off the children. Parents living away from the child should be referred to as "Dad" or "Mom" NOT "your dad" or "your mom." The latter sounds negative and seems to put blame on the child that they were born. Comments such as "tell Dad I'll pick you up at 6 pm" sounds so much less accusatory than "tell YOUR dad I'll pick you up at 6 pm." It might be semantics, but because respect prevails it does positively change the level of emotion heard by the child.

Complex trauma describes children's "exposure to multiple traumatic events." These events are "severe and pervasive" and can disrupt a child's development.[2] The effects of complex trauma or having many ACEs are long lasting. The same divorce, handled differently, can be traumatizing. If the children experienced chronic stress like unstable housing, domestic violence, physical and emotional abuse, or if they are forced to have alliances with one parent or the other, the stress level may be higher or result in a complex trauma.

The way a person bounces back from trauma depends on the experience. A prolonged level of serious stress can result in a slew of developmental delays, sensory deficits, challenges with bonding, and much more. Trauma can manifest itself in behavior problems, academic challenges, medical and psychological ailments, drug or alcohol abuse, or gang involvement. This is what some children are trying to work through and why it is crucial to understand what parenting a child with difficult behaviors is all about. Understanding which kind of emotional baggage the child carries is the goal.

Through our experience and training, we have been taught to manage out-of-control behaviors in children; this is called trauma-informed parenting. I think for years the information I learned went in one ear and out the other until one day I had an epiphany about the effects of childhood stress on childhood behaviors. The revelation was that trauma (often unknown) IS what causes a lot of the extreme reactions a child exhibits and why they escalate so quickly.

For example, saying "no" to a treat at the grocery store checkout line may seem like no big deal to some children; they can easily move on with their day. Others fall off the deep end over it. Of course, part of the child's response has to do with a lack of parental follow-through where having a tantrum in the past caused the child to eventually get what they wanted. But let's put that aside for a minute. If you put the non-fussing child next to the fussing child, it may be that the fussy child has witnessed abuse, neglect, or other trauma in their life, and that actually affects how their brain interprets the limitation of the candy. In short, they are experiencing actual physical brain changes caused by trauma, and this is spilling over into the checkout line situation.[3] The child may literally lack the cognition to realize it is just one treat on one day and that life goes on. Understanding how the brain senses what is happening is a huge part of managing the plan to effectively parent different reactions in children.

I do not excuse poor behaviors in children, but I became a much better parent once I understood this important concept. Before knowing this needed background information about why a child might operate in an emotionally chaotic way, you may have been inclined to judge the mom and child at the store thinking that the mother has no control over her child and that the child has no control of their emotions. This is not always the case. This is why every person needs to understand trauma and how it affects the brain's response to stress.

If you are fortunate enough to parent a child with no trauma or behavior problems, then you may instead think about growing your knowledge base. This will help you process why some of the neighborhood children or classmates of your children act in ways that you are not familiar with. After understanding the big idea about stress and trauma on the brain, we can start to parent our children better.

A CHILD'S POINT OF VIEW

Let's start with a very young child's point of view and consider how they process and understand what is happening around them. When they are out of their comfort zone, babies and toddlers feel trauma and loss in their own dear little ways. Verbal explanations cannot always effectively help them understand when they feel nervous, scared, and fussy. I think that the effects of sudden change are seen right away when they are, for example, placed in foster care. They are forced to get used to everything new all at one time, and they have little understanding of why life as they knew it has suddenly changed so drastically.

Our little foster daughter Ella came to us at five months old. For months, she had been left alone for long periods of time. Her mom strapped her in a car seat with a large bottle of formula propped in her mouth while she went out in the evenings to participate in adult activities. This baby had to drink or drown. A neighbor finally called children's services enough times with complaints of the mother leaving at the same time every evening and hearing the baby fuss for hours that the authorities removed Ella from her mother.

When Ella came to our house, she was grossly overweight from spending long periods of time inactive in a car seat and had a slew of untreated medical conditions. The facts of the case that I am aware of show many trauma points. Ella suffered from neglect, abandonment, poor nutrition, and later we discovered evidence of physical and sexual abuse. Ella's stressors were real, and she exhibited behaviors not typical for her age. She did not want to be held during feedings, did not seem to enjoy cuddling, had very limited fine and gross motor skills, and showed very few emotions with her facial expressions. She did not babble or even coo, which are activities that most children five months old can do. To help her through the transition to our home and the many new sensations she was likely experiencing, we sought excellent medical care, monitored feeding time, and provided soft music, swaddling, and cuddling. She qualified for and received speech, occupational, and physical therapy. Since she spent so much time strapped in a car seat, we encouraged tummy time play to help build her muscle tone so she could begin to hold her head up on her own. Her social worker worked directly with Ella's mom to decrease her dependence on abusive men for her livelihood and to help her find better daycare options. I worked with her to increase her knowledge of proper medical care and of growth and development for her child, all in support of Ella's basic needs.

For preteens and teens, the effects of trauma are seen in a wide range of poor behaviors. They might have extra big complaints in just about every avenue. More than usual teen behavior, they may have dramatic mood swings, extreme emotional outbursts, and exhibit physical violence. Low self-esteem, poor judgment, and overwhelming feelings of depression can all be triggered by stressful or traumatic events. Their sense of reality or pain can be warped too. How this age group manages their stresses depends a great deal on how they have been taught to cope. Here is where good parenting helps.

We accepted a group of five siblings (fourteen, eleven, eight, and one-year-old twins) years ago. This was an especially difficult placement because we were having to parent a teen, a tween, an elementary-aged child, and babies. The self-control behaviors were nonexistent. We witnessed screaming, the silent treatment, physical aggression, and offensive language directed at us. Each of these children had suffered varying degrees of abuse and all were severely neglected. In addition, the mom (along with her current boyfriend) and the three dads were not interested in working together with Ron and me to get the children's needs met. At a minimum the children needed proper medical and dental assessments as well as their schooling levels evaluated. The only way to help these children survive all this unsolicited change was to focus our mindset on what each child's point of view was, what they individually needed from us, and how we could plant a few seeds of age-appropriate behavior change in them in the time they were with us. We knew they had been set in their ways for a long time and they would most likely be returning to the same setting, so we used our energy to heal their physical wounds, attend to their deplorable dental conditions, encourage nonaggressive expression of needs, build their self-esteem, and teach them as many safety concepts as we could manage. With the older three, we identified their natural talents and taught a few basic life skills. We will never really know if any of this helped them, as four months later the courts decided to send them home and we do not hear from them. As their temporary parents, we pray that the children will remember some of the lessons we taught regarding health, self-control, safety, and motivation.

One baby girl, who is now school-aged, had many residual effects from her mother's severe drug abuse during pregnancy, another type of trauma. As a baby, she suffered from extreme drug withdrawal symptoms that lasted the better part of a year. Currently, Jessa has attention issues, is socially immature, and has many academic delays. Thankfully, she is now being raised in a family who knows how to support her needs through family counseling sessions, attentive medical care, holistic foods supplied by their family farm, and special instruction at school.

From Jessa's point of view, life is hard. Her personal history includes suffering many traumas—from a lack of prenatal care and being born to a drug-addicted mother to difficulties in school—but she also seems to be getting the foundational support she needs for her continuing life journey!

PLAYING DETECTIVE

Children have a labyrinth of needs, some known and others unknown. Parents are the detectives observing the children's behaviors and trying to get a feel for how to best help them. Children do not come with directions, and frankly until there is enough knowledge in the parents' skill bank, the child's needs can be confusing and overwhelming. We need formal training to get a driver's license, but little or no training to parent a child. Only time, experience, and critical thinking skills will help us mature in our parenting abilities enough to read what each child's needs are.

Some children who have poor behaviors are affected by undiagnosed medical needs that are not understood by their caretakers. Other children have obvious needs that have been ignored. The first step in parenting is figuring out which needs are specific to your child and getting to work on the most serious ones right away. So many children can suffer from genetic conditions, insidious ailments, or mental illnesses that no one has investigated and that may be contributing to poor behaviors. Get the child evaluated by a medical doctor and then progress on to a specialist, if recommended. While physical delays are fairly easy to recognize, invisible impediments such as cognitive, emotional, or mental health issues take a lot more investigative work to identify.

I often hear from new parents that once they left the hospital and took the baby home, they had the thought of "now what?" Parenting is piecing together the child's needs while fitting your life in as well. Adding to the complexity, caring for children other than your own means putting in an extraordinary amount of time coming up with an appropriate order of needs all without having a complete background history to draw from. So before starting new parenting techniques, address the medical factors first.

I ran into a new foster mom recently who had just completed her first foster placement with a seven-year-old boy. She had that "deer in the headlights" look about her as I inquired if the placement went well. She hesitantly started to reply how emotionally exhausted she felt with the whole foster-parenting situation. I asked her if she was surprised about the degree of the child's medical obligations and hidden needs. She readily agreed as tears began to stream down her cheeks. She explained that she had no idea how neglected his healthcare was and how much investigation, catching up on appointments, and lost hours of employment they were expected to endure before they could even begin to look at the developmental and behavioral needs of the child. Any parent can empathize with how helpless and overwhelmed this family felt being thrust into this new situation. I encouraged her to remember that any needs she did successfully address for the child were more completed pieces of the puzzle than before he entered their home.

We have seen this scenario ourselves many times. One- and two-year-old siblings who came to our foster home years ago had not been taken to routine checkups. The drug-addicted mother was barely getting by with minimal food, a broken-down vehicle for shelter, and car seats as beds. There was a huge list of what her young children needed. As in this case, whenever I get new children into our home, I focus my efforts on helping them feel comfortable and safe and then tend immediately to their medical needs. Every single medical need a parent meets makes the child feel better. No matter how small the intervention feels to us, this good investigation of their needs keeps advancing the child physically and emotionally.

More than just successfully surviving the exhaustion of each day, parents who have a good understanding of the effects of stress and trauma can then start the hard work of helping a child enjoy their childhood rather than be overshadowed by their past.

CHAPTER 2: NUTURING LOVE

Children thrive when surrounded by love and support that uniquely fit their needs. Active parents use layers of love and kind discipline to teach their children to respond to challenges with self-control. The parents' ultimate goal is to help their children draw on the skills they have been taught when they face a challenge.

LAYERS OF LOVE

Layering a child with love is a mindset that reminds a child that they are important to us, and we will not leave them to face their challenges and traumas alone. Instead, we will teach, guide, and help them work through tough situations to find a solution that will be in their best interest. Layering a child with love includes endless different techniques.

As parents, we seek to meet the needs of the child through the lens of building them up—to positively nurture them through childhood into adulthood. My thought is, if you raise well-adapted children, then one day they will be self-sufficient functioning adults. Children who crumble in the face of adversity face a harder life ahead, whereas those who have good coping skills to draw on can have the confidence to pick themselves up, learn from the experience, and move on. Layers of love give the child those skills.

When children grow into adulthood having learned healthy coping skills, they are able to figure out appropriate resolutions to problems. As an added bonus, we, the parents, will have a calmer life too. Sadly, I know elders who never got the chance to relax as they hit retirement because they are busy raising younger generations of grandchildren, bailing adult children out of endless binds, or are still financially supporting others. There is a time for full-time child-rearing, teaching, and being financially responsible, but there should be an end date too.

Tre and Gabby, who are currently twelve and eleven, are two special children who lived with us as babies long ago. After foster care, they were adopted by a wonderful forever family! The layers of love these children have received through the past decade include benefiting from an agency staff that stuck with them through a long and drawn-out case plan, a successful adoption with a family who already had another biological brother placed with them, and extended long-term support through our family. The children, who simply call us Aunt Kathleen and Uncle Ron now, have had consistent emotional support from all these angles as they have grown. They still come back to visit us often, and we anticipate we will be part of these children's lives on some level forever. That is effective layering of love.

In my experience, children who have behavior issues have often missed out on being surrounded by layers of love at an early age. Layers of love are meant to decrease a child's frustration and suffering and increase their comfort and growth. When a child has stresses such as an unstable living arrangement, persistent academic struggles at school, undiagnosed medical conditions, inconsistent caregivers, *or* caregivers who are inconsistent in their expectations of the child, it often leads to stress and confusion for the child. Behavior problems often result. Layering a child with love brings about stability, better coping skills, and reduced stress.

Simply put, this is making as many actions as possible in a day about loving, teaching, and building up but also not rescuing them from every one of life's inconveniences. In our society, we are robbing all sorts of people by taking away the opportunity to learn from mistakes and the satisfaction of hard work by promoting endless victimization and free giveaways.

Recently I watched an interview of a young able-bodied man who had recently aged out of foster care at eighteen. He said he wanted off government assistance more than anything and wanted to be in control of his life and to be able to support his own small child. He had the earnest desire to jumpstart his journey into responsible adulthood. In this interview, he sought a job opportunity where he would make enough money to also cover the cost of childcare so that they could meet their goal of being financially independent. I hope there was an employer out there who saw the news story and who could provide this layer of love for this young man. Genuine support for a child, or a young adult for that matter, helps them heal from the stresses of the past and builds their momentum to become independent adults and functioning citizens.

Parents must also teach unsolicited thoughtfulness from a young age. It feels right to be good to others, not because someone is going to honor you for it but because it is teaching an individual how to see outside themselves. Even small acts of kindness layer someone with love. Positive interactions help us all feel strong. In the realm of parenting, helping replace bad memories with good ones adds layers of love, padding the child for a bad day when a layer might be stripped away. The idea is to build each other up.

Seventeen-year-old mom DeAnn was a great young lady who was placed in our care. While she needed layers of love teaching her parenting skills and supporting her career interests, she was fantastic about passing out layers of love too. She was a sassy but sweet young lady who was mesmerized by foster care and what was going on all around her. She wanted to know details about parenting, how to be a good provider, plus a hundred other things. She laughed at the antics of the littles in our home and joined in with mimicking my skills as she learned more about her own childcare style each day. She said she loved being here amongst the activity and fun energy in our home. There is no reason that layers of love can't go both ways!

ACTIVE PARENTING

In addition to layering a child with love, the concept of being an active parent is very important to learn when nurturing a child. Being physically fit is not what I am referring to, but a state of mind.

Active parents want their children to grow, learn, and discover something new every day. They talk with their children, explain the world around them, and listen to their point of view. They talk about everything from nursery rhymes and spelling words to independent living skills and faith building. A great deal of energy and time is devoted to being an active parent, and adopting clever parenting ideas helps teach children to be accountable for their decisions and to think through situations before they act. This effort promotes positive self-esteem and is rooted in self-discipline.

Eventually we want children to take over the responsibility of correcting their behaviors independently.

Active parents know that through their conscious, strong parenting style they are building up their children with confidence, grace, and self-control. Active parents do not let other falsehoods raise their children. In short, we work to build a child's self-esteem with as many true and positive interactions as possible. In our home, we simply downplay negatives, kindly correct behaviors, and guide with positivity. After a while, active parents live this lifestyle effortlessly and raise well-disciplined children with few behavioral problems.

The opposite of active parents is inactive parents. Inactive parents expect the responsibility of raising well-adjusted children to fall on someone else. They blame teachers when their children are not smart enough, the nosy neighbor for calling children's services, and the authorities if their child gets into trouble with the law. Their general mantra is to look elsewhere for their children's formation, when in reality they need to look inward.

Inactive parents are more passive with their children compared to active parents. They rely heavily on computers, TV, and video games to entertain their children until bedtime is near. This breeds socially immature children who have fewer life experiences to draw on because their life experience is being built by some form of media. Bringing children into the world means taking the time to raise them.

One evening, at our favorite local restaurant, the waitress who knows of our foster-care work rolled her eyes at me as she sat a family with four youngsters down to eat and they all pulled out their own individual tablets with earbuds to watch different shows while their parents scrolled on their phones waiting for their dinners to be prepared. This was such a missed opportunity for the parents and children to interact socially and create a good memory of going out to dinner together.

Active parents stick together and support each other's efforts because we are all trying to find clever solutions to ever-changing problems that arise. We share what seems to work the best. Active parenting strategies help children learn to turn away from bad choices and repeat positive ones instead.

KIND DISCIPLINE

Fear and pain never help a child to grow in positivity. Using kind discipline that is meant to teach and not harm will more successfully help parent a child. Unfortunately, many children in our world have experienced such terrible discipline practices that we can hardly imagine. Honestly, thirty-five years after taking in our first foster child, I am still astounded with the stories the children tell me about being tortured on purpose as a means of control and severe physical punishments as a means of "discipline."

Abuse and neglect are not forms of discipline! Neither helps improve a child's ability to thoughtfully control their behaviors. The longer Ron and I are foster parents, the better we understand the long-term implications that abuse and neglect have on children. We have learned a great deal from children in foster care and how they have mightily survived these horrible traumas.

Within the walls of our home, we want to care for and protect all children in any way we can. The issues of the court system and proper punishment of the perpetrators are not in our control. What *is* in our control is the ability to push the negative incidents to the back burner of our minds and to not let them consume us. We trust that the authorities will handle that aspect of the child's life as we focus our parenting strategies on tenderly caring for the needs of the child. The hard part of foster parenting is choosing to be an active parent for someone else's child whom you did not ignore or neglect but are trying desperately to heal.

Some parents have done a miserable job protecting their children and providing for them. That leaves someone else to pick up the pieces. Kind discipline counters the effect of unkindness and works if the child knows they are safe and that the expectation goalposts are not always changing. We have seen this quickly evolve into better self-control for the child. Using kind discipline that is designed to teach and not punish takes time and effort, but it is also immensely satisfying to see a responsible child emerge. Being a heavy-handed disciplinarian is neither appropriate nor necessary.

During one intake night, I was helping bathe a little boy named Omar who was four years old. As I always do, I discreetly checked for any skin anomalies to properly report and document. It didn't take me long to notice a triangular shaped scar on his thigh. When I asked him what it was from, he told me he wasn't listening to his teenage cousin who was left in charge to babysit him. As a result, the cousin took a hot iron and burned him as "punishment." Unfortunately, the burn penetrated through his jeans and down to his skin too. This not only caused a severe physical scar but also a lasting mental one for him. Obviously, this teenage cousin did not have effective parenting skills to fall back on to properly correct Omar.

Clever parenting ideas, like layering a child with love, being an active parent, and using kind discipline, eliminate so many problems before they start and will lead to better self-regulation in children. We want children to know they can get to the point that they do not need their parents looking over their shoulder as their conscience. After all, in young childhood the parent is the main influencer of the child, but in middle and high school, peers and the media step into the picture as well. We want their foundation firm to give them the best advantage to make good decisions at this point in their lives and beyond.

CHAPTER 3: BUILDING A STRONG FOUNDATION

Children desire to make a life for themselves that they are proud of. Oftentimes, the situations they have been given are not their fault, and their behaviors have been learned as a result of their unstable circumstances. Once we begin to help them move on from their past, we can work toward building a stronger foundation.

TEACHING NEW HABITS

Teaching children to unlearn negative habits and build new ones toward the goal of a stronger foundation is the never-ending life work of a parent. Negative habits can occur because of situations not under our control while others are because we have let our parenting skills falter. The first step to improvement is having the desire to see change; this means it is not too late to start building new habits. Habits that center around good decision-making and appropriate responses enhance a child's foundation. Children need to feel secure that their home is their soft place to land and their strong place to take off from. They will come back many times for reassurance.

Some children's parents are aware of the advantage of teaching good habits in physical, emotional, and social health from the start. But often with children who display difficult behaviors, good habits early in life have not been taught.

One basic thought when teaching new habits is knowing the appropriate role of the parent. This means the parent has to be grown up enough themselves to assume the adult role. Some behavior problems in children happen because the roles of the parent and child are not clear.

Parents should lead and guide their children toward self-control and therefore, over time, lessen the need to be a watchful eye hovering over the child's shoulder. Confidence grows when they can make age-appropriate decisions on their own. It is not the job of the child to lead or for the parent and child to be best friends. Once the clear and proper roles of the child and parent are established, then other techniques can be added to continue the training of the family. I promise it will become easier to parent those children who are challenging you once this proper relationship is established.

Ron and I have seen a child's fears and anxieties immediately comforted by reteaching what a parent should and should not be doing. This wave of relief frees up mental energy for the child to work on these new habits we are trying to build.

Four-year-old Ava was skittish and nervous about anything happening around her. A simple suggestion to tidy up her play area before coming to eat dinner would disproportionately be taken by her as the weight of the world being placed on her shoulders. She was constantly being too hard on herself when truly we understood that she was just learning. We worked with Ava to build her resiliency and joy and to help her understand that we were just looking out for her and asking her to follow the same rules that all the other children were following. She came to know that we were trying to help her fit into the household routine rather than criticizing her choices.

Many children have emotional walls of protection built up around themselves that are hard to penetrate. Children are of many different races (ethnicity or nationality) and cultures (personal ideals and morals), and they are all unique individuals who hold beliefs near and dear to them. We are happy to allow children's own ideas, but that does not change our rules as the adults in our family. Carefully and caringly listening to children's opinions and wanting to incorporate their ideas without losing the beliefs of the parent is the goal. This is how we make every member feel valued and keep the family strong at the same time.

As children learn new habits, they start to feel safe and let their guard down, realizing they are allowed to expect safe discipline. They will learn that discipline is based on clear guidance and that they will not suffer abuse or neglect. They can then more easily start to build new habits in other areas of behavior knowing first that they are in a safe environment.

TRUST

Misbehavior can be triggered from past distrust, so we work on building up a child's trust level. Little Andie would throw an arm up in a shielding type of move or back away when she was startled by an adult moving too quickly toward her. This was a natural reaction that she often had. A simple action of raising a hand to brush the child's hair or reaching over her head to grasp the refrigerator door handle could bring on this type of recoil because of the abuse she experienced in the past. We have learned to play down that type of response and not react with excessive emotion or questions. We would simply remember the next time to say "I am going to brush your hair now" or "Excuse me while I reach over you" instead of assuming that she knew what was happening. Our hope was to retrain her brain away from that automatic guarding response and put her at ease.

As in any home, once children begin trusting, the parents can move on to establishing rules and structure. For example, respect for authority from parents, the police, or the court systems happens naturally for some children but not for others. We know that opinions differ widely based on their experiences. Some children have had police officers play basketball with them at the park and hold the door open to greet them each morning at school, while others have watched the police arrest a loved one. Respect for authority can be skewed, but most children are aware that they have benefited greatly from police and firefighters in their neighborhoods.

Foster son Alan was brought to our home late one night by a police officer in a squad car. Now this is a bit unusual because children removed from their homes are usually screened at a children services agency first, but because of the circumstances this evening the officer brought him to our house directly. Earlier that day, when the police arrived at his apartment answering a domestic violence call, he had been told by his parents to run out the back door and hide from the police. He did, and he stayed hidden in the neighborhood for hours. His little sisters were all placed in another foster home, but Alan had not yet been found. Once he got cold and tired, he went to a neighbor for help, who then called authorities.

For some reason, they couldn't get ahold of the foster mom where the sisters had been placed, so we took him in for the night until communication with the other home could be reestablished. The officer was very kind and had a warm personality. He took Alan for a burger and fries on the way to our home, visited with us in our living room while Alan got acclimated, and by the end of the transfer process, Alan decided he trusted the police. He even told the officer he wanted to join the police force when he got older so he could help children who were "really scared" too.

Sadly, because someone along the way has told them differently, we are faced with reteaching some children even bigger trust concepts, like the fact that every person in the world is just as worthy and important as the next. Six-year-old Lanny repeatedly said "I ugly" or "I bad" whenever he was sad, mad, or frustrated. It was his go-to response for coping with just about anything. We assured him that he was as sweet and special as anyone else. This defeated little one needed so many layers of love wrapped around him to build his self-esteem because the verbal and physical put-downs he was subjected to in his young life were so ingrained. We would hear on occasion, "I good?" and immediately reenforced this glimpse of self-love.

MODELING

Along with building new habits and establishing trust, demonstrating active parenting through modeling is another way to raise a child with a strong foundation. Children have a need for positive, low-drama role models who practice what they preach and cheer them to success. In our situation, we try to be good examples to both foster children and their family members. We do this by saying less and doing more. If children see that the adult is unkind, lacks control of themselves, and does not follow rules, they will not either.

Most of our foster children's parents are young themselves, so our demeanor and example will be learned by them as much as by their children. Moments of disrespect definitely happen, but we strive to be calm and mature and to model polite behavior anyway. We do this not only for the adult we are facing, but for the child who is likely nearby watching. Children are great imitators; give them something great to imitate.

Preschoolers Jacob and Lyndsey were a set of siblings with a particularly difficult mother. I would drop the children off at the visitation center for their weekly visit, and the mother would be in my face with her chronically bad attitude. She had many complaints ranging from the color of clothes her children had on to having to ride the public bus system to get to the visit center every week. On several occasions, agency staff would demand that she back down and move away from me. Her children picked up on her rudeness. I reminded myself that I was not the reason her children were in foster care nor was I the reason she was angry. I dug deep to maintain composure and modeled calm behavior in front of the children, allowing them to witness a situation where I refused to be drawn into her adult temper tantrums.

Four-year-old Lyndsey actually apologized to me one day through her tears for her "mommy being so mean." She seemed ashamed and embarrassed about her mother's behavior. That is not a situation a small child needs to be put in. The mother missed out on an opportunity to, at a minimum, keep her temper in check and model restraint in front of her children.

FOLLOW-THROUGH

Another mighty pillar of a strong foundation is follow-through. Every other strategy that active parents use is built on the premise of following through with what has been modeled and said to the child. Consistent follow-through greatly reduces the need for most other disciplines because children will know that you mean what you say because you follow through every time. When parents are kind yet strong in convictions, childhood behaviors will improve. Pick one sentence that simply and clearly states what you want from them. Do not be drawn into distractions like emotions and complaining.

Our ten-year-old foster daughter Karen routinely refused to complete her math homework. Acknowledging that school was a struggle for her, I told her, "Once you show me that you have completed your math homework, then you may get your paints out." If I chose to get mad and yell, she would completely shut down for hours and hours of misery toward all those around her. When she argued or talked back, I said in the same matter-of-fact voice, "Once you show me that you have completed your math homework, then you may get your paints out." After many sessions of yelling, moody pouting, and blankly staring at her computer screen, she finally learned to take the ten minutes needed to complete her small daily assignment and get the work done. I simply noticed with a smile that she did a good job completing this task and handed her the paints. It took *well over a year* of consistent follow-through for Karen to understand this follow-through concept.

Now don't get me wrong, I have had incidents of high intensity through the years where I badly wanted to give in to a pouting child, but I did not because it only makes it worse the next time I need them to follow a direction, and that is not fair to them. On the other hand, I do believe in changing my mind. If my first request was too hasty, I then say to the child, "I changed my mind, not because you cried about this, but because once I had a chance to think about it, I decided my request could be more reasonable." It is good for children to see that we as parents are not perfect and make mistakes too.

Parents who lack follow-through, are inconsistent with their requests, or who give multiple warnings have children who do not know how to behave on their own. If extra warnings are given, then why should the child ever respond on the first request? The person giving the extra warnings is undermining the follow-through idea and sending mixed messages to the child, adding to their confusion, and likely increasing the incidence of poor behaviors.

I was in Florida visiting the hotel pool and witnessed an exasperated mom tell her two school-aged girls to get out of the water "now or we are never coming back to the pool ever again!" The mother begged, pleaded, and bartered with the girls for close to an hour. Finally, after giving two-time extensions past her original request, she got very angry and cursed loudly at the children, prompting them to get out of the pool. Later that evening, while waiting for my son to finish his lifeguarding shift, I went to the pool deck a second time and all three of these family members happily marched back in for another swim. Poor mom, she just did not get it, but her children sure did.

INDIVIDUALIZED PARENTING PLANS

We strive to take excellent care of children in our home according to their individual needs and abilities. I call this our individualized parenting plan. An IPP is our family's organizational plan to care for a specific child. These plans evolved out of necessity to meet our personal goal of providing each child who passes through our home a successful foster-care experience. Families could benefit from establishing an IPP for each child in their care.

A great beginning step in making the individualized parenting plan for each child is to base it on the most accurate background history. Remember to use other sources to piece together information when caring for a child. In foster care, the information we get initially is vague and merely the tip of the iceberg. So, ask different people who know the child: grandparents, should you see them at a visit; a counselor at the child's school; or the check-in nurse at the doctor's office. Every piece of missing detail can help formulate better parenting plans for the child's care. Talking with the biological family can sometimes feel elusive, "like sewing feathers together," I always say, but I stay dedicated to getting as many facts correct as possible.

This theory impresses upon parents that children are very different from each other, even within their own families. All children need individualized parenting plans that support their weaknesses and boost their strengths. A few years ago, we had three twelve-year-olds placed in our home at the same time, followed by three two-year-olds the next year. None was like the other in their age group! These twelve-year-olds were so different from each other in confidence, social skills, maturity, and schooling. The two-year-olds had similar medical needs, but their emotional and physical development were grossly different. Still, all interventions and disciplines are meant to teach; they just have to fit the right child at the right time. That is where the IPP helps.

Take the twelve-year-olds Cheyenne, Kaye, and Kathy for example. Cheyenne was adult sized, but due to her extreme levels of trauma, like spending long days locked in a cellar, she craved silly childlike attention. She talked in a baby-type voice, slept with a night-light on, and wet the bed. I would put her social maturity around seven years old. Kaye was the silent type, introverted and sullen. She excelled in some areas of academia and was well liked at school but was neglected and physically looked like a very small, malnourished child. Kathy was outgoing, socially promiscuous, and had an expectation to be seen and treated like an adult. She also had the grandiose idea that she ran my house. Their IPPs meant different supports, different styles of communication, and definitely different disciplines to fit each child's personality.

Now for the darling two-year-olds. Skye lived here first before the twins were placed later. She was developmentally delayed and fed completely by a feeding tube placed directly into her stomach. She was sweet and had a calm demeanor about her. Unfortunately, she was pretty sickly when she came to us, so we attended many different doctor appointments to address her medical conditions. Skye's mother was much more attentive to Skye's needs, once she fully realized what they were. We worked closely together to keep Skye healthy, well supported, and bonded.

Twin Abby was mobile, ate on her own, had some beginning language skills, and leaned toward a typical two-year-old in her development. Her sister, Emma, had a temporary nasogastric feeding tube but took some food orally as well. She was nonverbal and just beginning to crawl. Dealing with many stomach-related issues made her uncomfortable and fussy a lot of the time. The mother of these two was not involved in the case, and they were headed for an adoption. One "fun" fact was that they all wore glasses, and they thought it was the funniest game to swipe each other's and switch them around, multiple times a day. Oh my goodness, those little girls! They kept me on my toes!

We allowed the pre-teen girls to pick activities and rewards they were most interested in and that supported their personalities the best. Cheyenne was an animal lover and spent a lot of down time with our self-proclaimed therapy dog Jack. Her immature behaviors were best dealt with by keeping her close to the center of the family hub and ignoring as many inappropriate behaviors as we could. Time spent alone in her room was scary for her, so any variation of time-out was never implemented. Kaye needed limits set on her alone time with a heavy focus on socialization skills at any opportunity we saw with her. Kathy needed to be relieved of her imagined parenting duties and encouraged to just be a kid. I passed these helpful hints along to any caretaker helper in my home and also to whomever came after me in their life journey, whether that was their parent, a relative, or an adoptive family. This helps them with continuity of care and stability.

For the little girls, the IPP included many lists! Feeding instructions, type of feed, tube care, leg braces, colors of glasses that correctly went on which tot, medication administration schedules, and a dozen other details. These were important to keep me organized, make sure the right child was given the right medication, and to help with transition of care when I wasn't around.

Lastly, we had two teen moms, within weeks of each other, placed with us along with their children. They were the perfect example of some children who are self-directed and self-disciplined while others have little momentum of their own. DeAnn was a self-starter. She took her childcare upon herself and readily asked me when she needed help or wanted me to take over her mothering duties for a while. Rae was a slow mover. She spoke slowly, moved slowly, and had trouble thinking things through. She needed me to tell her what her listless baby needed and took very little initiative. Talk about two very different IPPs! Of these teens, I was grateful that DeAnn was the one bestowed with a high level of energy and enthusiasm since she was raising twins!

By building new habits and seeing poor behaviors improve, parent and child relationships are strengthened. When we and our village of support understand the importance of building a strong foundation, we will help children improve their behaviors. The best any adult who cares for children can do is plant many seeds of stability in the hopes of grounding the child in good habits that they can carry into adulthood with them.

CHAPTER 4: "THOUGHT"FUL PARENTING

Children surely do encourage us to think creatively! When one idea falls short, we must adjust our strategy and think of a new way to guide our children's behaviors, helping them understand what we are teaching and why. I have gained a wealth of knowledge from friends with children, from reading books, listening to podcasts, and utilizing trial and error, yet I am still stumped at times! I have to change my way of thinking and go outside of the box to come up with a new strategy to try the next time.

LISTEN

Most children want to be agreeable. Listening to their concerns, instead of reacting to their behaviors, can make all the difference between rational problem-solving and an emotional blow up. Children are not always looking for someone to solve their problems; oftentimes they just want to know they can talk and be heard.

How children process what is going on around them can be skewed due to their past experiences. Since children are as unique as their issues, actively listening to what a child is worried about or excited for, instead of always having a response ready, shows the child that they are worthy of our time. When we put our phones down, we can better listen to the child rather than half-heartedly hearing through the background distractions. We can then parent the child by guiding them as the conversation progresses.

In our home, we make an effort to listen to why a child chose an action instead of assuming we know what happened. Since these children come from different backgrounds, we automatically stop before we judge or scold. Doing so gives us an idea of their side of the story. Things are not always as they seem, and children become frightened easily if conclusions are reached too quickly; this is when communication shuts down and behaviors escalate. Not always, but sometimes children truly do not know that what they did was wrong.

Five-year-old Jabril was caught at the checkout with a small toy race car in his pocket. He gave the car back to the manager and apologized but said that his mom told him they needed that particular car. The racetrack at home was missing the car and if he ever saw one, he was to bring it home. He explained that there was a difference between stealing the car because he wanted it, which he knew was wrong, and stealing it because he needed it. We listened to his rationale. Obviously, we had to do some reteaching that stealing is stealing, but his resolve was firm that this is what his mom had told him. Children are often street smart and need exposure to positive sources to guide them socially and emotionally.

Our eight-year-old foster son Franz was caught stealing directly from his teacher's purse because he wanted to draw pictures for his classmates and family on the colorful sticky notes he saw inside of it. We had to teach Franz what is socially acceptable and that there are ways other than stealing from his teacher's purse to go about getting the drawing supplies needed.

Over the years, listening to children's thoughts for why they do the things they do has been an incredibly eye-opening experience for us—and one that has changed the way we listen to and parent our children. Still, we want to help the children understand that stealing or falsifications will bring only short-term satisfaction.

Listening to the family the child came from or other influential adults in the child's life is important too! For example, not all words and gestures mean the same thing with every family! In one family they call the little toddler sister "Mama." The whole family—her siblings, her mother, even her grandfather—calls her this. In another family, we referred to a four-month-old as "the baby" and the parents were sincerely offended, insisting that she was a big girl and should be treated as such. "Capping" to one set of teens meant lying; to another it meant quitting. DeAnn's family described her babies as "greedy," which she explained meant they had healthy appetites and were growing into healthy children. Growing up, we did not use the word greedy as a compliment, so this was new to us!

Sixteen-year-old Darcie was placed with us along with her infant son. It often seemed like she had little to talk to her son about; however, every time he passed gas she made a big dramatic deal about him "farting" saying "you gross, you gross." It was the comment she seemed to make to him the most, as if she didn't know anything else she should talk to the baby about. We suggested that she ignore the normal baby tummy occurrence and say "good baby work" to her son, and smile at him. We also suggested that she talk to him about numbers, letters, animals, and the sounds a truck makes. We explained that these are positive ways for her to talk to her son and increase his language and vocabulary skills and that emotional bonding is strengthened by looking him in the eye and cuddling. She learned that these were forms of communication her infant would enjoy. In the future, she will likely want him to speak to her respectfully too.

I also had two sets of teens from the same geographic neighborhood that used similar expressions in different ways. This happens because cultures exist even inside cultures. I repeatedly heard the comment "he hittin'" and wasn't sure why this was causing some verbal upheaval between the two sets of siblings at my home. So, I asked them to explain it to me. One set told me it is in reference to drug usage and "mom's nasty boyfriend," and the other set told me they were referring to physical abuse. The teens were upset with each other because of what they thought was being said about their families. I can't stress enough to earnestly talk to the child and the people they spend the most time with so you can understand what you're hearing and not misunderstand their dialect.

As the years go by, the slang children use changes too. Some words are made up and learned through social media. One day a child told me school lunch was "mid." What does that mean, I wondered! After further clarification, he told me "mid" meant that the food was just okay. Another set of children told me that they "smolder" at the kids in their class. When I asked them to demonstrate that to me, they turned their mouth up with a side smile. These are all expressions I am quick to ask them to explain to me so I can remain current with the slang and understand them.

Words and expressions gain traction because the influencers online are using these phrases as regular language. As more people view online content, the more the words become integrated into society and socially accepted. Older generations might be left in the dark on these words and ideas. We may have to ask someone we trust to explain what we are hearing so we don't have the wool pulled over our eyes. But that's ok – we all have our gifts.

THINK BEFORE YOU ACT

Listening helps us plan which action to take next. There are two different thoughts on "think before you act," or emotion regulation, as a parenting technique. The first is that not all child behavior needs adult intervention. Adults must think before *they* act and let the children settle some disputes on their own. As parents, we can take a step back and wait to see how the situation evolves. Standing by and watching children launch their own problem-solving techniques is appropriate. On the other hand, some children severely lack any level of negotiation skills, so the adult may need to intervene and help the child think before *they* act.

Especially for small children, downplaying small infractions and ignoring negative behaviors is the simplest and easiest technique to curb their bad decisions. If the incident is miniscule, such as pulling a toy out of another child's hands or changing a TV channel without another child's permission, parents do not need to feel obligated to jump in with a scolding. Instead, we can ignore the negative choice and allow the children to solve the small problem on their own, only stepping in if needed.

Children can bring some unusual problems to the table because not all have been brought up in an environment where they have learned age-appropriate problem-solving skills. Emotion regulation is not a skill we are born with, but it is best developed early in life. Some children slug first and talk later. Honestly, though, I am not against this altogether. One of my kindergarteners came home from school with a reprimand for slugging a boy on the playground. The written warning explained that the first grader, who had been bothering my kindergartener for quite some time, approached him from behind and punched him in the head at recess. In an immediate reaction, my younger child swung around and instantly slugged the older one back. While I do not actively encourage this method as a solution, the older child never bothered my younger one again.

In most cases, our thoughts move to instructing the child to regulate their emotions by pausing for a moment, taking a deep breath, and thinking for a split second before they act, teaching that the choice they make will have a consequence. Having children stop whatever impulsive action they were contemplating and pausing momentarily seems simple, but it is a monumental developmental task for most children. The delayed ability to master this idea is the basis for many behavior problems. This technique takes consistent, patient practice and will need to be repeated again and again.

There is strong scientific evidence that children's upper-level brain functioning (pausing before they act) is often underdeveloped in children who have experienced abuse, neglect, and other developmental delays. In other words, children who suffer abuse and neglect or other trauma show evidence of the effects it has on the wiring in the brain.[4] Their past experiences are essentially about survival, so flying off the handle occurs long before they ever have time to think of the consequences of their action. Take heart, learning to calm their impulsivity can be taught.

Five-year-old Viktor, who was diagnosed with autism, threw practically every toy he came in contact with. He had to have many reminders of safe play because of his extreme impulsivity. He had suffered a great deal of abuse and neglect as well as abandonment early in his life, which likely also contributed to his developmental delays. We worked very hard day after day to get him to pause, breathe, and think before he acted. One day, we saw his anger flaring over a sharing incident with his brother, Josh. From across the kitchen, I watched him stop, take a deep breath, and wait a second. He growled at his brother that he was mad and that he wanted the toy back "in one minute!" I was shocked that he used words! A child simply deciding not to clobber his brother can be the highlight of parenting some days.

Think before you act should be taught and expected by every member of the home, but remember to judge according to the individual's ability. I was out with my friend the other day who was able to correct her thirteen-month-old son Kane from pushing and running ahead of the other children and to wait for his turn. I did not expect him to obey her. I was amazed that he was calmly able to understand his mother's

60

request and was proud of his mom for her obvious consistency with follow-through when parenting him. This was a pretty amazing feat for a one-year-old child.

BRAIN DRAIN

The "brain drain" technique will help with those behaviors when a child does not listen to directions.[5] From time to time, children will obviously disagree with what you ask of them. They may whine, cry, or barter in response to what is asked. I have heard, "C'mon, the other kids are going," or "Why not?" or "You're not my mom." Children would prefer that parents justify their answers, and this drains the parent's brain. Children of all ages naturally brain drain parents by asking the same request over and over, in hopes of wearing them down, even though they have already been provided an adequate explanation. The parent response to the brain drain tactic allows children's antics to be easily combated.

The most effective way to fight the brain drain is to simply turn the idea around. Do this by picking one sentence and repeat it back in a respectful way. Teen Topher was a big sports fan. He wasn't so big on cleaning up after himself. He always wanted to be attending the next school function. My response would be something like, "No problem, we will head out to the ball field once the popcorn has been swept up." The teen might reply, "My mom doesn't make us sweep at home," or "You get paid to clean." If I bothered to respond at all, it would be the same sentence: "We will head out to the ball field once the popcorn is swept up." Some children get the unspoken message—that I am not going to change my mind—right away, while others will try several more times. We do not engage in the child's comments, emotions, or attitudes in their attempts to brain drain us back, and we do not divert from our original request. Instead, we stay calm in the use of our chosen sentence and wait patiently until the sweeping is completed. Once a child consistently experiences parents who aren't phased by the brain drain, the need for repeat promptings diminishes.

Eight-year-old Maya, who likes to bake, would hear, "The muffins can be started once the dishwasher is unloaded." In the beginning, I had to repeat myself often, but as she settled into this style of parenting, she completed her chores faster because she knew the request and the timeline would not change. It is a thrill for parents and children to understand this technique because it makes the home calmer and more enjoyable. Eventually, if I stick to my original clearly stated request, the children will decide to obey, or else their activity will be delayed or possibly canceled altogether. It gets easier over time.

POSITIVITY

While ignoring a child's negative behavior has merit, embracing positivity is wholeheartedly rewarded. Siblings JJ and Nadia used to have a severe shortage of food in their home. They ask for candy every time they come back to visit us. We happily say "Sure, let's decide together when the best time to eat the treat would be though." We might agree to after lunch, for a mid-afternoon snack, or as dessert, but they are still allowed to pick the candy out of the basket when they ask for it and put it up on the counter. The children heard a positive response to their request for a treat and I got the time for consumption I preferred. Positives all around.

Eye rolling and huffy attitudes are sometimes best ignored because the more a child knows a behavior bothers you, the more they will do it. Seven-year-old Frankie had turbulent emotions where even the slightest infraction against her feelings was met with big emotions, clenched fists, shaking shoulders, and sobs. We pretended not to see her frequent breakdowns and went on with the conversation, not drawing undue attention to her because we knew the loss of her own control truly bothered her. Frankie's counselor taught her to take deep breaths, count to ten, visualize relaxing her hands, and how to regain composure again. Frankie knew that she was old enough to not have these fits and was embarrassed when she lost control. Our part of mitigating the behavior was to not draw attention to her while she took a moment to gather herself. We also encouraged a lot of outdoor activities with her because being in nature seemed very calming for her. I turned to self-preservation mode for a few minutes, if needed, usually by walking down the driveway to get the mail or to the garden to grab a strawberry, which gave me a moment to catch my breath too. As we met back up, we both were usually ready to get on with our day. She was the cutest and nicest little girl, and it was sad to see her emotions get the best of her in this way.

Parents trying to curb negative behaviors need to start by listening to their children and help them learn that they will be heard. Children are less apt to overreact to small infractions against them because their frustrations are lower when they know an adult will actually listen to them. Quietly ignoring the negatives and accentuating positives builds confidence and leads children to better decision-making. These techniques used together teach children to be more resilient, self-regulated, and have better behaviors.

CHAPTER 5: GROWTH FROM THE INSIDE OUT

Being a conscientious parent is hard work and takes a great deal of time and energy. Clever ideas come from careful scrutiny of the problem we are seeing and being willing to try more than one approach while we are learning each child's personality and go-to coping styles. Since I do not have all the answers, I know that it is necessary to ask for help and to remind children that it is okay for them to ask for help too.

HURDLE HELP

"Hurdle help" means assisting a child through a task before they get overly frustrated. It is the act of lending your strength instead of reminding them of their weakness. I use this frequently. School assignments are a prime example. While we want to let children work through assignments on their own, we also want to prevent them from becoming so frustrated that they feel defeated before they get started. No lesson is learned when the child is overwhelmed and simply crumbles in the face of the assignment. Some children seem to be able to complete assignments independently and easily, whereas others need additional help to know how to even get started. Hurdle help is the boost that instructs the child over that one confusing step and gives them momentum to get on with the rest of the assignment.

Ten-year-old Tina had numerous learning disabilities. She suffered from poor medical care, severe malnutrition, speech delays, hyperactivity, persistent truancy, and physical abuse. She needed hurdle help to keep her frustration manageable so she could attempt her assignments. It took many weeks of encouragement getting her to sit in a chair for more than ten minutes at a time, to finally have a desire to learn the lesson. We persisted with our one request that she try her best to read the directions independently first and then we would review them a second time with her to make sure she understood what was being asked of her. She cried and cried at first but later started having small successes on her own. Her confidence grew. She actually was not a bad student after months of one-on-one attention and hurdle help. Starting assignments on her own occurred and she edged closer to grade-level work every day.

From the child's point of view, they are saying "I'm struggling," but from a novice or frustrated parent's point of view there is a lack of the child trying. Remember that traumatized children, or non-traumatized children for that matter, don't always act their chronological age. In my opinion, Tina acted more like a six- or seven-year-old who was not getting her way. Years into my parenting career I am better able to understand the fact that some children have undiagnosed disabilities, which might be preventing them from completing age-appropriate tasks. I learned how to easily adjust my parenting techniques to hurdle help each child.

Tina needed calm patience, a structured work area, and just a bit of guided help. Having learned coping skills—such as asking clarification questions, focusing her thoughts, and limiting distractions—she defaulted to fewer stall tactics and was better at getting the assignment started. The change doesn't happen overnight, but with consistency small steps were made. Mercifully, she started blooming in both her maturity and schoolwork. We were happy for her newly found successes, and this helped boost her confidence. Over the year she spent in our home, her reading level and grades greatly improved, and her self-esteem soared.

This makes me think back to the days when I was a school nurse. One class in the school had both a girl with diabetes and a boy with epilepsy. The teacher had her hands full monitoring these two children and their medical symptoms as well as tending to the rest of her students. After I provided some education on their conditions and on the physiology behind what was happening after the girl's blood sugar level was off or the boy had a seizure, the teacher better understood that each student needed an adequate recovery period in order to be physically and mentally ready to sit for classwork again. The teacher thanked me for taking the time to help her over this hurdle—her lack of knowledge regarding her students' conditions.

REMOVE YOURSELF

There are appropriate times to "be there" for a child and times to remove yourself from the presence of a child choosing to act poorly. Separating ourselves from the problem at hand and allowing another authority figure to correct the situation can be another useful plan of action. As parents, we teach children good decision-making and then let them put their learned skills into practice. If the child makes a poor decision, such as hanging out with the truant teens at school, I must let the school staff reinforce the rules and give the appropriate consequence. Their punishment supports my corrective conversation at home and all adults are using teamwork to reinforce each other. We remove ourselves from any power struggle by refusing to engage in arguments surrounding the choice the child and the peers have made at school and support the school staff in their discipline measures.

Sometimes, children will try to maintain control of what they can and may not want your advice in changing their ways. Sleeping, eating, temper tantrums, learning, actively participating in counseling, and choosing friends are all examples. Spending time preparing supper does not ensure that the child will eat. Providing a teen with quiet time for homework is controllable, but making them read the textbook is not. Having children settled in their rooms at bedtime is enforceable, but making them go to sleep is not. A child can be driven to school but cannot be made to give the energy and effort to participate.

We remove ourselves from attempting to control these aspects of another person's life because it is a waste of energy. Instead, we choose to influence the environment surrounding the situation and encourage their good decision-making. For example, I cannot control whether my foster teen skips class, but I can control whether she is free Friday night to "just hang out at the mall" with the crowd of truant-influencing friends. I may strategically fill our Friday night schedule with a family outing to the local football game where I can keep an eye on the teen, should she choose to gather with friends, rather than leaving her unattended at the mall.

I can take my spunky six-year-old foster daughter to her family counseling session each week, and even if she sits there staring imaginary darts at the counselor for an hour, we will still go every week as scheduled not only because it is court mandated that she attend with her caregiver but because I don't want her to be in control of the situation. When she starts questioning me on her timeline for going home to her mom, I will remind her that her part in her family's case plan is to attend AND participate in family counseling and that I doubt the reports the counseling staff was sending periodically to update the judge were giving her high scores for effort. I know her participation is something I cannot control, but I also know I don't need to put myself in the middle of the problem either. Eventually she will figure out that she does have some control over helping her family strengthen, and I will remember that I am doing everything I can to help her overcome not seeing the value of counseling.

One teen, Dollie, was particularly challenging with her moodiness, negativity, and dishonesty. We were emotionally exhausted trying to be active parents to her argumentative personality. Because we were struggling with our patience, we once had to phone a friend and take several days off, removing ourselves as her caregivers. Our dear foster friends happily suggested that Dollie could join their family on "team demolition" at their house for those few days. Among helping with many small children in their foster home, they had spring yard cleanup and gardening to do. She learned how to repair wall damage, tear old wallpaper off kitchen walls, and paint meticulously so that the project looked beautiful when it was done.

We avoided a grounding situation, removed her from our personal space for a few days, allowed her to learn some home maintenance skills, and remained cheerful with the other children placed with us while on our mini vacation from

Dollie. Dollie was not present at our house where she would have likely spent her time being rude and disrespectful. When she came back, she was a transformed girl, stopped asking for a new foster-care placement, and cheerfully appreciated us more.

STAND YOUR GROUND

Being a registered nurse, I am used to most medical situations. There are times, though, when I do not feel comfortable with a child's needs; we have heard the same concerns from other foster parents too. It is not always popular, but there are times when we must assess the situation, realize that we do not know the answer, and insist on going to professionals for help.

Our little six-month-old foster son Nick had complex medical needs that were not clearly understood initially. We needed to take him to many appointments with specialists for their assessments to provide us with a rudimentary understanding of the level of medical care he needed. At one point, I took him to the pediatrician three times in five days for persistent vomiting and respiratory difficulties. Finally, I took him to the children's hospital emergency room, and after they assessed him, I started hearing comments from the staff about "continuing to keep an eye on him at home." I firmly expressed to the staff that I respectfully refused to take him home that night. Eventually, a kind doctor ended up admitting him for observation. I stayed that night with him, and his oxygen level dropped to 13% (this is not a typo; 96-100% is normal) within a few hours of getting to the admit floor! He was transferred to the pediatric intensive care unit immediately and did not leave again for thirty-three days! In my opinion, he would have likely died in our home that night. I had to stand my ground that evening and not let anyone bully me into something I knew I could not handle. Thank God, Nick is alive, healthier, and thriving at home these days.

On the flip side, there are times when it is appropriate for a child to stand their ground as they mature in their thought-processing and decision-making skills. Teen Darcie and her infant son were brought into foster care over an unstable housing issue. As her eighteenth birthday approached (when she would age out of the foster-care system) and planning started for her to go to a women's shelter, her biological dad gave resistance about the move. I was proud of her as she stood her ground and told her dad that she thought it was the right move for her, as she could get daily life coaching, finish her GED, and find assistance to help her obtain stable housing. Her maturity had improved, and she demonstrated the ability to weigh options so she could make the best decision.

CHAPTER 6: EFFECTIVE DISCIPLINE

Discipline comes from the Latin word *discipulus*, which means student. When parents use discipline, it should be to teach, as you would teach a student. Straightforward discipline helps children grow through guidance. Children cannot be held responsible for unpredictable behaviors when all they know is an inconsistent environment. Being an effective parent means focusing our thinking on our vast experiences and then deciding which action to take. Always try hard to consider the child's upbringing, resist snap decisions, and focus on teaching.

NATURAL CONSEQUENCES

Choices and consequences give children a chance to practice being responsible for the decisions they make. As parents of a small child, we give choices to the child that they will be able to handle, and we are happy with the outcomes of the choice, whichever they choose. As the child grows in age and maturity, showing more competence in their decision-making, we start to relinquish control and allow them to make bigger and more meaningful decisions on their own. This is how responsible parents help their children mature and develop.

One set of siblings (Michael, seven; Zoe, five; and Beau, four), whose mother was recently deceased from a drug overdose, were coming to our home until their father was discharged from the Army. The discharge process took longer than expected, and the children were with us three months instead of the anticipated three weeks. Our goal for these children was to move them from a place of immaturity and unruliness to one of maturity and order. We did this by having them make many choices every day: "Would you rather clean toys in the house or out in the yard first?" "Do you want to set your school clothes out before or after your bath?" "Once you go home, what will be the best way to communicate to your dad that milk and toothpaste need to be bought?" We felt that instilling a sense of order and calm in their lives would be very helpful for their dad, who was already needing to adjust to losing his wife, becoming a single father, and transitioning back from Army life overseas. Every intervention utilized to decrease the children's sense of chaos and increase their sense of calm is helpful to the stability of the family.

A foster mom we know was parenting fourteen-year-old Tim. His general mantra in life was "I'm no good, I'm just a thug." His experienced veteran foster mom took him on a long walk to a cemetery one day near her home, where they noticed the ages of the deceased on the tombstones. She had a candid talk with him about making choices to move himself toward success, including finding more appropriate adjectives to describe himself. She told him, "Whatever you think you will or will not become, you're right." She said this made an impression on him and he often spoke with her about how many of the dates on the headstones were near his birth year. They talked about the choices, consequences, and outcomes of the young victims' actions and how you can be sorry for a bad decision afterward but by then it might be too late.

Small setbacks from bad choices are a very important form of learning. Parents who deprive their children of learning natural consequences early on will impact how they will be able to handle responsibility as an older child. A college student who never woke up for middle school or high school independently because his mother was always taking the responsibility to do it for him will struggle waking up for classes in college. As a result, these choices, which would have had less serious consequences when he was younger, can have a big financial impact in loss of time and money if failing expensive collegiate classes occurs.

We took a trip to the community center one day, and our twelve-year-old foster son Andrew forgot to put his swim trunks on before leaving the house. As a result of his poor planning, he sat on the bench at the edge of the pool with his goggles and towel but no swim trunks. He did not complain about not getting to swim because he knew the first direction given to all the children that day was to get their swim suits on for the pool and then pack their swim bags. Apparently, he had forgotten. We resisted the fleeting thought of going home to get the forgotten swim attire. There was no drama or emotion. In fact, we did not even talk about it. We ended up having a nice chat sitting on the edge of the pool together while the others swam. The next time we went swimming, Andrew took responsibility to get ready for the pool and even asked his brothers if they had all remembered to put their swim trunks on. We complimented him on being an organized and responsible leader and had a lot of smiling faces that day when the swimming fun started again and this time everyone got to participate.

Another good example of a natural consequence happened when Dollie lost her set of earbuds on the bus. As a result, she had to live with the embarrassment of borrowing her little sister's princess headphones for a mandatory listening assignment at school. When she got angry, we expressed that we felt bad that she lost her earbuds and helped her brainstorm what to do about the dilemma. We helped her to think about checking the school lost and found and to ask the bus driver if he had seen them. Still, she owned the problem, and we did not solve it for her. At the teacher's suggestion, Dollie ended up earning credit at the school store with timely completed homework assignments for several weeks and "bought" herself a new pair of non-princess headphones. She took very good care of them after that.

We are not a punishment-based but a consequence-based home. We have found this to be better for the child's development and maturity. By letting the consequences do the teaching, the child will be led to self-evaluations and development of more cohesive thought processing. Short of "loss of life or limb," as one trainer always says, overmanaging a child sends the message that you do not think they can do the task on their own. So, allow independent decision-making whenever possible. The correct message we want to send is that all actions result in a consequence—good or bad.

MANIPULATE THE ENVIRONMENT

My favorite discipline technique is the old "manipulating the environment" idea. It is the granddaddy of techniques that makes life so much easier for parents! We have found that manipulating our environment helps us keep our children monitored and extra safe during their time in our home. We do not advertise to the children that we are creating a safe and public space for them to enjoy and play in; instead, we discreetly set up our home to meet these critical needs of the children without compromising their fun.

We use several play and relaxation areas in near proximity to the kitchen. This is on purpose because the adults in our home spend a great deal of time in this space. To ward off as many bad behaviors—such as general mischief, aggression, and physical altercations—as possible, we want children within our direct view. Keen supervision not only provides a high degree of safety but helps children learn that life can be less chaotic when they learn to steer away from constant negative behaviors on their own without an adult reminding them.

For us, taking in multiple foster children similar in age helps life go more smoothly especially when it comes to our designated play areas. We rotate toys and activities that all the children enjoy because the children's ages and interests are similar. We have fostered seven sets of twins so far because we have informed the agency staff that this is a situation that works well for us. Other foster placements we accepted that were close in age were sibling groups of seven, eight, and nine; eleven, twelve, and thirteen; and twelve, twelve, thirteen, and fourteen. Having several children in the same group allowed us to set up a highly visible computer area, outdoor gathering area, various sporting activities, and a craft table with scissors, glue, and paints, which were all activities that interested these children.

With little ones, we set up safety play zones to accommodate multiple sibling groups near the same ages. We recently had twins who were eighteen months old, so we cordoned off the sunroom and kitchen areas with baby gates, essentially making a giant two-room playpen. This setup allowed a safe and fun play space for the toddler-sized jungle gym set along with many gross motor push toys, and it kept the dog from eating their toys. The twins were safely in our direct line of vision, and they had many age-appropriate activities to choose from.

During the summer that COVID hit, we had two sets of siblings that totaled eight preteens ages eight to twelve at the same time. Placements of all older children helped us make the decision to get a medium-sized above-ground pool set up outside the kitchen window. I would not have considered a pool with toddlers in the house, but since all the children were about the same developmentally and comfortable in the water, this was an excellent time-guzzling summer activity. The children played mermaids, Olympics, and synchronized swimming and spent many fun hours on floats burning off pent-up energy. We think having age-appropriate safety zones increases the fun for the children, helps keep them out of trouble, and decreases the stress for us.

Because direct supervision is not always possible, we use a security camera in the basement playroom where most of our gross motor play toys are located. The children are aware that the camera is there, and they often run into the kitchen to watch the other kids playing on the monitor. We have a rule that an adult must be in the kitchen area so the camera can be seen when children are in the basement. Having this heightened intensity of supervision sounds extreme but becomes routine when raising children with unique needs.

I feel that bedrooms are better off not being used as play spaces or time-out areas for children. My rationale is that I want all children to interact with the family as much as possible. Not a lot of good comes from endless hours alone. Bedrooms are reserved for changing clothes, quiet reading, and sleeping hours, not as punishment space or play areas. Frankly, many children would love to be sent to their room for hours on end, but that would go against my belief in being an active and attentive parent. We encourage children not to pout in their rooms or dwell on discipline and to get on with their next activity as soon as the unwanted behavior has stopped.

A set of teens thought they could have a "girls' club" closed away in their bedroom after school. Topics of conversation would range from hate of foster care to dreading counseling to a dislike of their "creepy" attorney. We have found that endless hours of catty talk breeds negativity and hopelessness. While we wanted the girls to have time to talk together about what they were going through, we preferred these conversations to take place a hundred paces in front of Ron and me on our family walk where we could still keep an eye on the children but give them privacy at the same time.

DISRUPT THEM

We skillfully disrupt negative behaviors in a matter-of-fact way, preferably without the child realizing a parenting technique is in use. All of this is done quickly, calmly, and consistently, allowing the child to move on from their negative choice onto a positive one.

For example, "If you choose to throw the bat again, I will have to put it up." If the child throws the bat again, I will calmly walk over and without bartering or anger, take it and put it up exactly as I said I would. I let them know they can try again in a bit. Thirty seconds is enough time to disrupt the behavior. I would then ask if they would like to try again. One simple prompt about remembering how the toy is to be played with, what the consequences will be if the toy is misused, and consistently following through every single time gives the child direction on how they should act. If I am too busy to follow through, then the bat will be put up for the day. Also, if the child does a nice job following the rule, I will mention the positive behavior.

Effectively disrupting teen misbehavior takes a bit of ingenuity. Our biological daughter Elizabeth used to text me from college when she noticed an inappropriate song playing on the Alexa unit in the basement where our teen foster daughters hung out. As a clever way to disrupt the unwanted song, she simply changed the tune through her phone app to "The Wheels on the Bus." This interruption served as our signal that an inappropriate song was being played. The teens laughed hysterically, got the message, and I never had to say a word. Children learn that you mean what you say if you are consistent and do not change the rules.

DISTRACTION

Distraction goes right along with disruption and is a great technique to use to interrupt the negative moment and give the child a chance to get their attention back to where it is supposed to be. We immediately distract a child by talking with them and answering their questions about the difficult situation around them. We aim to keep children's frustrations low so they can unemotionally process what is going on and start to think about a proper response.

One night we took in a complex sibling group of five (ages five, four, three, and two-year-old twins). I have never witnessed such a need for distraction as I did late that night. They were screaming, spitting, jumping up and down on the beds, and literally bouncing off the walls. What was known regarding their level of trauma at home consisted of domestic violence, physical abuse, lack of stable housing, and malnutrition; plus it was late, and they were overly tired. This high level of activity meant dividing and conquering.

After an hour of peeling the children off each other, we worked to distract each with a snack and shower and then settled in bed. I would like to say we successfully read to them but that was a colossal mistake to even attempt because they ripped off covers and tore out pages before we knew what was going on. For an exhausting couple of hours, we used about every distraction idea we could think of to calm their manic behaviors and eventually get them to sleep.

REDIRECTION

Redirection is another strategy that active parents use. Redirection uses the idea of being cognizant of specific triggers for the child and then starting to intervene swiftly before behaviors get too out of control. If a child is actively monitored, it should be easy to recognize their individual signs of behavioral wilting before they become overly frustrated, act out, and need more time-consuming discipline.

LaMont had many disruptive behaviors, but he was also a good helper. He would frequently pick fights with another youngster when he was losing his self-control. Upon seeing him start to get irritated, we would move in to change the scene. We might simply prompt him by saying, "The kitchen trash is overflowing, LaMont." Because he had a helpful nature about him, he would usually stop what he was doing and go into the kitchen to empty the bag. This action prompted comments about how strong and capable he was to be able to pull the bag out, put it in the garage, and place a clean bag back in the container. He took pride in his ability to help Foster Mommy "all by myself." By this time, the frustration in the other room had long passed. LaMont gave many professionals a hard time at school and in counseling, but I think they concentrated on his negative behaviors too much and not his positives. He liked being "caught" being good; he just needed attentive redirection before he lost control. I can see genuine delight in a child's face when they realize they can make their needs known before needing to act out to receive attention.

Siblings Kyle (eighteen months) and Josephine (eight months) were distraught with being in foster care because they were so young and had no understanding of the system. They knew they were in an unfamiliar place with new people. The children were stunned and difficult to console (rightfully so!) during the first few hours at our house. We decided to set up a toddler-sized obstacle course, and our daughter, Elizabeth, crawled through with them until they got the hang of the activity. Kyle and Josephine loved this activity and were redirected to a happier environment. Before long, the little ones settled in, became more comfortable in our house, and played in their obstacle course often!

Eleven-year-old Avery started becoming emotional because her strong personality and sassiness were overwhelming playtime with the other children and tempers were starting to flare. I redirected her by requesting her presence in the kitchen to help me make snacks. This way her behaviors could be discussed and corrected away from the ears of the others. I asked her to choose between including all the children in the clubhouse play or having the playdate cut short for her. Then I followed through with what she decided. Children learn to appreciate calm intervention before their emotions become too much for them to handle on their own.

Disrupting poor behavior, distracting children away from what is causing the behavior problem, and redirecting their attention toward another activity decreases the need for further discipline. Parents use disruption, distraction, and redirection hundreds of times a day and probably aren't even aware of it.

TIME-OUT VERSUS TIME-IN

Time-out is a common discipline taught at all community parenting classes, but it is overused and minimally effective. When foster children are at visits with their parents, we try to help their parents decrease the use of endless poorly executed time-outs and instead guide them to briefly interrupt the child's infraction and redirect them to another activity. Bringing calm attention to the negative behavior quickly and quietly is more helpful than the child saying with exact correctness why they are sitting in time-out. If disrupting, distracting, and redirecting are used consistently, time-outs will rarely be needed.

If used, the time-out would be centered around interrupting the behavior, having the child process what they could have done differently to avoid the negative choice, and thinking compassionately about the person they offended. Time-outs, when we choose to use them, are kept short because we get bored with them, and we believe that children do also. Besides, more often than not, children will sit in time-out thinking about how much they hate you rather than reflecting on their wrongdoing. Instead of immediately banishing a child to time-out, we help them understand empathy toward the other child after an infraction. We might say to the one hurt, "I'm sorry you were hit. Are you okay?" We finish the brief interruption of negative behavior with a quick corrective statement to the offending child such as, "If you are kind to Gregory, he will want to come over and play more often" and a compassionate gesture such as a smile or hug to the hurt child. Both children will be asked to "go try again." Thus, within twenty seconds, the issue has been resolved, and we have prevented the need for a time-out.

Children who experience consistent discipline will know that they need to correct the behavior or a follow-through with another interruption of their playtime will soon occur. For children who refuse to alter their behavior after this type of infraction, we may use a short time-out. If the misbehavior happens again, the environment would then be changed altogether, and the offending child would move to a different activity in a new space.

"Time in" is a far superior discipline tool to time-out. Time in works by using coaching skills in combination with extra practice time for a child to achieve a skill. Children misbehave for a variety of reasons, such as lack of preparation, inconsistent rules, confusion, or fatigue. Active parents teach children HOW to act in certain situations. Verbal prompting about clear expectations ahead of time is referred to as time in because extra time is needed to teach the child proactively rather than disciplining the child after the misbehavior has occurred.

Say you need to take your children to a home-school meeting that you routinely attend every month. Last month when you attended, your children failed to listen properly and frequently interrupted. Try asking the host if you may come to the meeting five minutes early to "practice" good behavior in preparation of the meeting with your children. Explain to the children that you will be there five minutes longer this time because they need to practice getting settled and oriented to what is expected of them during an adult meeting. Children are smart. They do not want to go earlier than necessary. After the meeting is over, briefly discuss if the behaviors were more acceptable or not and adjust as necessary. Never threaten an extra time-in session or a time-out discipline without following through. Children sense weak parents.

HAVE A SIT IN

Being kind is more important than being right. For this reason, I rarely engage a teen in a heated discipline battle because the exchange usually becomes unpleasant and could potentially get out of control. So, I don't put myself in that position. Instead, I choose the calm and kind idea of the "sit in" discipline. This strategy works like a charm with preteens and teens. All I need is a few minutes of time and a large stack of paperwork to accomplish this technique.

When I see misbehavior escalating between teen sisters, I might say, "I'm starting to worry about your choices. People who cuss out each other don't feel good about themselves. All this gets them is negative attention." If this doesn't seem to help de-escalate the emotions, then I literally insert myself into the middle of behavior and have what I call a sit in before emotions get too far out of control. Making myself large and in charge by sitting down right in the middle of their gossip circle seems to take the steam out of the confrontation. Though their eye rolling is nearly audible, they typically are not looking to sort out their innermost feelings in front of me and usually move on with another activity.

Our adult daughter Melissa said this worked well for her one evening too when monitoring a middle school church activity. Several teens were interrupting the speaker and not being respectful of the students who were trying to actively participate. She informed me that she went over to the picnic table and settled in right between the two most chatty teens. She said the look of surprise and speechlessness was just what she was going for, and the church activity carried on after that without further interruption.

After I resorted to this technique a few times, the teens in my house learned to automatically stop their bickering as soon as I glanced their way and started gathering my work papers. They came to the realization that their sisters were not so bad after all, and they wanted to spend time doing activities with their peer siblings rather than spending time sitting next to their foster mom. Desperate times call for desperate measures sometimes. Eventually, they started internalizing the discipline themselves, and less tattling and more bonding resulted. On the occasion that the teens do want to talk, then I am all in for a little mother daughter bonding time and good conversation to solve a problem.

QUIET DOWN

When having a sit in fails me, I will try another approach by quieting my tone of voice. Speaking quietly to children is an important practice. A child's poor behavior choice does not need to be announced to everyone in the area. Loud, screaming children coupled with loud, screaming parents are an ineffective combination. Since adults are more at ease when addressed in a polite and calm manner, it follows that children must feel the same.

When it seems like behaviors are waning, consider getting down on the child's level and talking with them in a quiet and controlled voice. For instance, you could say, "I am disappointed that you chose to take the book from that little girl. Please give it back to her. We will pick another book to read." The child may not do much of what you asked in giving the book back, but quickly and quietly demonstrate as if they did. This will help avoid a full blowup while out in public. Hand the book back to the offended girl and begin reading another book right away. There is not a lot of time to form a big complaint, and desired reading is happening again.

Fifteen-year-old Bailey suffered from depression, anxiety, and low self-esteem. Because she was overly quiet, her brothers and sisters constantly spoke for her. We had to train them to resist the urge to jump ahead and finish sentences for her. While we think the siblings meant well, they were giving Bailey an excuse to hide behind them and ignore those who spoke to her, deepening her social anxieties. Since it took patience waiting for her to form thoughts and speak, we all had to learn to be quiet and curb our tendencies to speak for her. After a year of intense therapy, counseling, care from a specialty pediatrician, and an amazing teacher, she brightened some and began to enjoy being her own person and speaking for herself more often.

Speaking quietly to a child and saying things such as "It feels like you're upset with what is going on. What can I do to help?" I am amazed how often just those few kind words will de-escalate a potential problem. Even so, we cannot anticipate every action a child will take. A child may reject a quiet correction as an option, especially if past experience has shown them that an emotional scene will help get them the attention they are seeking. If I cannot prevent a scene from occurring, I can at least keep my own feelings in check, which keeps the situation from escalating.

TANTRUMS

Tantrums happen because the child is having a need met by the result of it. I have found tantrums with children to be fairly easy to manage. Keeping the child's past in mind and knowing the profound impact it has on the child's development, we are prepared ahead of time with techniques that will mitigate a tantrum from occurring.

When a tantrum happens with a child, I usually just sit with them, rub their arm or head, and tell them I'm sorry they are sad, mad, or frustrated. I just repeat that same comment until they are tired out, even if it takes a while. The next few times I will do the same because the tantrum is not likely about the fact that they only received a few cookies when they wanted the whole container, even if that is the chief complaint. It's probably more that they are tired and stressed with all that is happening around them and they shut down because they feel too overwhelmed to regulate their feelings at that exact moment.

Remembering to parent a child based on their emotional maturity NOT their chronological age, I try to move smaller children to a quieter area if I can and then start the calming-down process. If the child is schoolaged or above, we take the outburst as it happens. This is stressful, but if done well the first time or two it should stop because they know I will not give in to their demand, and they know the parameters will not shift.

One evening, we got a new placement of children in our home. My daughters had a choir concert at school that evening, so we took the new children along. The children— four, two, and one—seemed well behaved enough, so I didn't have any reservations about them sitting for a short part of the concert. We would sit in the back of the auditorium and have an easy escape route if needed. Thank goodness we did! When four-year-old Chris finished his snack, he immediately exploded in rage, demanding more. I honestly have never seen a child escalate that quickly. Ron swiftly scooted him out of the concert and did not give the tantrum any attention. We had no choice but to wait it out because this tantrum was not about chips but about being overwhelmed. Mercifully, the concert ended and we collected all our children and headed home.

On a couple of occasions, I have sat in the driver's seat of my car frustrated and mad, yet silent, because an object was thrown at my head during a child's tantrum. One time it was a shoe, another time it was a sippy cup. I try very hard to not get mad or react because that makes the situation worse, and my main priority while driving is to keep everyone safe. Also, the other children in the car will see that it got a rise out of me. Staying calm has two outcomes: It keeps us both from escalating, and it keeps the car on the road. The shoe thrower got his shoes removed every time we got in the car for several days, and the cup thrower was obviously traveling without a drinking cup now. These consequences last for a couple of days or until I feel sure they understand the gravity of throwing items in the car.

One time, our hefty eight-year-old Abe decided he was going to cry and scream at the grocery store because we were not buying every food item he wanted. He had been informed before we left home that each child could pick two grocery items to add to the cart that day. His mood had been wavering the last couple of aisles because he had already made his two selections and was unwilling to change them. By the time we hit the last aisle, he was mad at my "no" response for ice cream. He sat down on the floor in the middle of the grocery store and wailed.

Sensing that this fit was not going to pass quickly, I sat down quietly beside Abe, pulled a book out of the diaper bag, and began reading to the other children who were also along. I knew we would have to ride out this outburst because he was too big for me to move and correct elsewhere. I clipped my agency name badge to my shirt, identifying me as a foster parent. In my mind, this helps quell onlookers' anxieties that I was ignoring or harming the child.

After a few minutes that seemed like hours, Abe was embarrassed that I was not paying any attention to his behavior. At the very first sign of calming, I said, "Okay, looks like we are ready to go." I put the book away, schlepped myself up off the floor, and off we went. I accepted his mistake, and he did not have a scene like this again. I did not have to repeat myself to him many times after that day because he knew I meant what I said. His volume may have been loud and out of control, but my response and tone back to him were not.

I understand the hesitation that comes with downplaying tantrums, but with traumatized children this is the best approach if the goal is to build the child up emotionally as well as teach them they can't always have their own way. In polite society, they must be in control of themselves. Non-traumatized children may respond to other ways of handling a tantrum, but most of my experience comes from the traumatized child. Tantrums only continue to work for a child when parents bend and give in to what the child wants. Instead, we want the children to understand it's best to keep their stresses in check and that self-control is strength.

We make it our practice to avoid battles as often as possible but always follow through when we choose to participate in them. We pick our discipline carefully with each child and develop the best plan to quickly correct unwanted behaviors to help the child become more enjoyable to be around. Unconditional love does not mean unconditional acceptance of bad behaviors. As parents, we must be in control and not confuse anger with firmness.

CHAPTER 7: MANAGING EMOTIONS

It would be wonderful if there were a magic key to unlock the best way to teach children about managing emotions. Keeping our emotions under control is a learned skill. I had an amazing nursing professor in college who told our class that if your patient has adequate air to breathe and their heart is beating, we as the caregivers do have a moment to stop, think before we act, and figure out a good plan of action. Like all experiences, letdowns, and even tragedies, managing emotions is the key.

HANDLING DISAPPOINTMENTS

When parents demonstrate how to react maturely in response to stress, children get a reliable reference guide when they are faced with adversity themselves. Having viable alternatives decreases the need to fall back on explosive outbursts to get attention. Self-regulation and accepting responsibility can be excellent opportunities for growth. Often, we learn and remember more from a mistake.

Near the beginning of our parenting time, we had a teen foster daughter, Candace, who fluctuated between being distant and withdrawn and agitated and aggressive. We tried to help her cope with the mounting disappointments of life, but she struggled to embrace any new coping mechanisms. Unfortunately, after only three months, she ended up in the hospital to treat her schizophrenia (which we were previously unaware she had been diagnosed with) and a month-long admission where she was eventually discharged to a residential facility for teens.

More than a decade later, Candace called us out of the blue! She wanted to tell us that she liked being part of an intact family with an employed dad, a car that worked, groceries in our cupboard, and that beloved beach-themed bedroom she had decorated. She recalled how much we encouraged her drawing and drafting skills in school. She told us she had gotten her mental health issues under better control, was attending counseling every week, and was currently employed with a computer company. She said she also had found a church to belong to that offered a drug dependency support group. Candace, a teen I would have never betted on being touched by our brief time together, said she kept the vision of our family in her mind and knew that was what she wanted to strive toward even in the midst of all her hardships. That special call one Sunday afternoon was exceptionally reassuring as a parent.

Sharing with your child an experience of how you handled a situation where you were embarrassed or failed is also a great way to help them feel like they are not alone in their struggles to handle disappointments. In that same nursing program (different professor), I suffered a big letdown with my anatomy and physiology class. While I studied very hard, I earned an 89% (a B) for the class. I tried so hard to get that elusive 90% because I wanted an A in that heavily weighted ten-credit-hour class. This was an upset to me and one that I share with my children from time to time. In the end, I excelled in my career as a nurse, even without that A. As a mom and foster mom, I still use many of the skills I learned during that class and all those years of hospital nursing. This story helps me teach the children about keeping a lifelong perspective after a disappointing event.

One time, we took a set of siblings who were going to be staying with us for two weeks as a short-term respite placement. A few days previous, they had come into foster care and had been placed at another foster home, but the foster family was leaving on an already-planned vacation that weekend. Not knowing that these new children would be coming into care, they were unable to take them along on their vacation. These three siblings—Theo, Diane, and Teddy (seventeen, ten, and four)—were already dealing with coming into foster care, then they found they could not go on the trip everyone else was excited for, and they were told they had to go to a respite foster home in another city for two weeks. Talk about emotions!

Theo was so disappointed and withdrawn when he got to our home. We felt terrible for him. Diane and Teddy were intrigued enough with our toys and playroom that they seemed not to care as much about feeling left out. At first, Theo was quiet and kept to himself. Understandably, he didn't want to take the time or energy to get to know us very well since he would only be with us for a short time. After a few days, Theo would go outside and shoot a few baskets with Ron and some of the other children. Finally, as the second week approached, he decided he would try several outings with the family.

He went to the library with us one day, worked out at the YMCA another day, and spent a whole day out with me one-on-one. I took him to the store where he picked out new tennis shoes (men's size fifteen!) and then went out for a double cheeseburger for lunch. When we got home, Ron found him a set of superhero movies he wanted to watch. At the end of the movie trilogy, he told us, "This was the best day of my life." Teens have many pent-up emotions that can be difficult for them to share, but patience and spending quality time with them goes a long way in helping them adjust.

ANGER

Oftentimes when a child does not get their way or experiences disappointment, they can become angry. We were very grateful that this gentle giant, Theo, was able to keep his warranted feelings of disappointment from moving into anger. Of course, not all children can do this. There are angry days in every type of home, and children see how adults handle themselves when upset. Children will follow our temperament and look to us to see how we are handling rising anger.

More than once, I have been driving foster children to the agency for visitation with their family when I received a call to turn around and go home because the family had canceled the visit at the last minute. The children obviously are upset and often become angry, which I know will seep into the rest of the day and probably the week, until the next visit. I feel bad for them.

The kindest way to get through these real feelings is to help them learn to manage their anger until it passes, instead of lashing out. I can say something like, "We go to the visit center each week on Tuesday hoping your mom and dad will come, but as you know, it does not always happen." We would discuss their emotions if they wanted and then go into what is happening for the rest of our day. I would likely give the child a fun choice of some sort to get their mind off the disappointment. I may say, "Let's get lunch out, and when we get home you can decide if we do chalk art on the driveway, get the splash pad out, or go downstairs and use the punching bag for a bit." We do not overdramatize the situation but instead care for the child's emotions and teach them proper outlets for anger.

Our foster half siblings Drue and Louisa visited with their respective dads once a week fairly consistently in the beginning of their placement in foster care. As often happens, the fade in attendance begins and the dads showed up fewer and fewer weeks each month. At first, the children cried and yelled with anger at missing their daddy time. I choose to never lie to a child as to why the visit is canceled, though I do make sure to explain in an age-appropriate way. I explained to the five- and six-year-old children that I was sad for them that their daddies did not come because I know they have been let down. As the weeks and months wore on, their reactions dulled to an eye rolling sigh, and the sulky emotions passed more quickly. Eventually, the children stopped asking about their dads' visits.

We still included their dads in various conversations, prayed for them, and had pictures of them in the children's memory books. We emphasized that even though their dads will always love them, they could not take care of them and that is why they lived with foster parents. It became a matter of fact over time, and the children learned to cope with the anger.

With teenagers, I often must remind myself that they are mad at the situation and that they really aren't mad at me. But my husband puts limits on how much pouting he will allow in the house and will say something to them if their emotions start turning into disrespect. Ron is a tolerant man toward the children and what they are going through, but he does keep a close eye when it comes to them pushing the impolite envelope. Usually, getting a ball game or some other activity started with him will ease the misplaced tension.

EMPATHY AND HOPEFULNESS

Empathy and hopefulness are some of the hardest emotions to instill in a child. Our little seven-year-old Libby was crying one evening. When I asked what was wrong, she said, "I can't sleep without my mommy and daddy." I gave her a hug and told her I was sorry she was feeling sad and how hard it must be for her to stay in foster care. When I looked up, one of our older foster sons, Tre, had come over to pat her on the shoulder and said, "It's hard for all of us, Libby, but remember foster kids have lots of mommies and daddies and sisters and brothers who love them. That makes us lucky too."

That small act of genuine empathy from our sometimes rough twelve-year-old made her smile and still brings tears to my eyes. Tre's sister Gabby joined in the conversation and asked Libby if she wanted to sign her name on the dollhouse club member roster and started a sweet play session of house where Gabby told Libby she would take care of her. There is no way to solve their giant worries, but we can at least be good listeners.

We work hard to show that positive moments in a day create hope in life. It is hard on the children to only have discipline, sadness, and loss to focus on. My grandmother used to say, "This too will pass," with a gentle pat on my hand because she knew that life continues around difficult days. Sometimes no one has ever taught a child to consider finding joy in the journey of the day. The idea is not to downplay their feelings but to instill hopefulness in them.

We advise children to feel grateful and to see outside themselves. Just because people choose to be cheerful does not mean their burden is light, it just means they have learned to find joy in their work. We believe the degree of resiliency and joy the person has correlates to the amount of grace they show in their day-to-day life. Being hopeful is a conscious decision and one that needs a lot of maturity to choose.

We had a little three-year-old foster daughter years ago who was neglected and physically abused at her home with her mother. Onna was quiet and withdrawn. She did not smile or talk much. In fact, she used to grimace in a mad way more than anything. She did not choose to play with other children. Over the next eighteen months, she ended up going to several different types of therapy through the schools and at our local children's hospital, which forced more time with peers. With these services, her personality came to life. Her favorite type of play eventually became playing mommy to her baby dolls. If she was not dragging three of them around all at once by their legs, then she was rocking and cuddling them singing in their ear. I was glad to see her empathy develop with her excellent "mommy care" for her babies. It was touching to see some hopefulness blossom in this little girl.

CHAOS

Chaos is an energy-draining emotion. Some children are living in conditions of extreme chaos so it's no wonder their behaviors reflect that. Disrupting the chaos restores order and allows for fewer emotional ups and downs. Active parents spend a good deal of time helping control the chaos that surrounds the child.

When new children come into our home, the first couple of weeks can be incredibly difficult. There are so many new details presented to their brains all at once. The car seat they are riding in does not feel like theirs. Their special blankie got lost in the shuffle at the agency and the new clean one does not smell right. The food doesn't taste like the kind of food they are used to. There is a dog in the house and maybe they are terrified of dogs. The endless list translates to feelings of uneasiness for the child.

Having multiple changes coming at them from so many different directions is overwhelming. This is why many children are often out of control when, hours after being removed from their family, they finally make it to us. When I say out of control, I mean running around in circles nonstop, banging their head against a wall or the floor, swiping items off the counters, turning over furniture, peeing on the floor, or gagging and vomiting at will. I try to explain the reality because I often hear that "children in foster care are just like other children that need love." While this is true to some extent, it also is not.

Children who have many layers of confusion or disbelief to work through have to start with calming the chaos first. What calm looks like for that child is another detail we must figure out. Starting with simple explanations about where they are, what is happening to them, and getting them to use an actual bathroom are our initial focus. Following house rules, doing their best in school, or having a conscience for right and wrong are a long way off. We must be realistic in our expectations.

Parents who are high-strung, loud, and chaotic in their personalities typically raise children who are the same. We saw this in four little children—ages four, three, and one-year-old twins—whom we raised for about a year and a half. When the four would have their parents visit at the visit center, the children were loud, boisterous, and rude. They did not listen to their parents' or the social worker's directions. But, one week per month, the paternal grandmother visited too. They were changed children when she was there. They waited in turn to speak, played in a more cooperative way, and were respectful to others around them because grandma expected this of them. The children clearly knew how to behave when she was present. This matriarch's stern love for her grandchildren was a force to behold!

Environments full of chaos where rules are constantly changing breeds inconsistency with how the child learns to react. One set of toddler siblings we fostered were used to staying up late. According to their mom, the children slept with a TV on in their bedroom. They also slept in till noon because that is the schedule Mom wanted them to be on due to her late-night lifestyle during the week.

On weekends though, her schedule was different. She needed the children to get up early so she could make it to her part-time job in the fast-food industry. She complained constantly how her children didn't sleep well, behaved poorly, and were out of control, but really the small children were probably confused about what was being asked of them. Understanding that there are seven days in a week and which day is which is unreasonable for most one- and two-year-olds. In reality, this is a parenting issue not a child behavior problem. At first, the children were confused with our consistent 8 pm bedtime and 8 am wake times and no TVs in the bedrooms. Eventually though, they adjusted to the consistent environment and were much easier to have around because they were well rested and understood what was expected of them.

PRAISE GOOD DECISIONS

Praising children who make good decisions and catching the children "being good" is great parenting at its core. An occasional comment such as, "I like seeing you share your birthday treat with your sister" or "That was kind of you to let your brother choose the movie" are simple examples. We praise a child's efforts in situations like these where they thought independently to do a kind deed without prompting. Reinforcing positive behaviors rather than always criticizing negative ones is refreshing for both the child and the parent!

Focusing on day-to-day accomplishments helps heal emotional wounds, and it passes the time with good thoughts instead of dwelling on bad. Displaying schoolwork on the refrigerator, announcing a student of the month winner at suppertime, or a big brother yelling "way to go" to a younger sister's first successful two-wheeler bike ride are tiny sentiments that help build up each other. My personal favorite is enthusiastically participating in youngsters' magic tricks. Giggling at the "mysterious disappearing pencil trick" makes their day and is a simple way to support the child.

Karen was absorbed in a perpetual state of raging emotions. Her high-strung chaotic personality was exhausting for everyone around her. Thankfully though, she had an excellent counselor whom she liked. The counselor helped her work on the importance of slowing down and finishing what she started, seeing the worth in herself and others, and working toward a more positive life experience. She went on to find a love for journaling and different art projects with her counselor who taught her (and us) that allowing persistent negativity in one's life directly correlates to why emotionally unstable people go through many disposable relationships. The counselor worked with Karen on emphasizing a lifelong need for hopefulness and gratefulness in relationships. Over time, these changes brought a nice degree of calm into our home.

An added benefit to parents who generally speak in an emotion-controlled style is getting a big response from their children when they are forced to use high emotion, as in the case of safety. Yelling "stop" or "no" warns the children that something urgent is happening and they can easily understand that the warning requires their immediate attention. This could be a life-or-death situation. More than once, a car was speeding recklessly down the street near where our children were playing, and we were forced to yell to keep the children safe. Because I save big yelling for emergencies, the children did not hesitate to listen to my warning.

A scene in the *Little House on the Prairie* series illustrates my point. While helping with chores in the barn late one night, Ma Ingalls told Laura to go inside the house. Laura obeyed her mother without asking any questions because she could hear the serious tone in her mother's voice. Once the family was safely inside, Ma explained that she had a sternness to her voice because there was a bear in the pen with the cow!

Had Ma talked like this all the time, Laura may not have been quick to listen. Since the urgent tone was only used in emergencies, the children listened and were safe. This is a perfect example of why we select our tone judiciously.

CHOOSE WORDS WISELY

Just as we choose our tones wisely, we must also choose our words wisely. This is a great parenting technique that allows the parent to ask questions that encourage children to think for themselves instead of putting them on the defensive. We are not trying to change *what* they think but rather teach the children *to* think. This perspective has an amazing effect on children's lives because some children have repeatedly heard abusive and degrading words and we want to counter that negative experience with as many affirmative words as possible. This in turn allows the child to let the role of the victim fade, gives them power to move on with their own lives, and is a big step in trauma recovery.

Instead of thinking for the child by saying "do your homework," we would make a comment that allows them to do the thinking and be in control. For instance, "Feel free to do your homework when you're ready but before the TV goes on." Other thinking words such as "Let me know what you decide about needing new shoes once your closet is cleaned out," "Keep me posted on how you are liking your counseling group," or "What are your thoughts about going to the football game on Friday night?" are also often used. Choosing open-ended phrases to communicate encourages children to think first, acknowledge their feelings or wants, and then give their opinion. We always offer choices that we are willing to uphold and steer away from ones we less prefer to be picked. We want to keep our word to them.

Sometimes, children need adults to advocate for them. For example, children coming into foster care typically have the disadvantage of being transferred in and out of school districts, so making friends is hard. To help with a smooth transition, we speak carefully to the teachers and school counselors as soon as a child comes to our home. We fill them in about the ever-present friend concern and we see if the assigned teacher can identify a student or two in the class who might have a similar interest as our foster child. Our hope is that the teachers can smooth the way and initiate a friendship to help ease the child's worries. After a few days, we might ask the child, "How is the friend situation at school?" or "What is your take on your class?" We advocate for the child's social needs, communicate the issue to the school, and then hear the child's take on the situation. By choosing our words wisely, we are guiding a situation but not solving it for them.

I will add here that institutions and agencies need to choose their words wisely also. Not only do children learn from what they hear and see around them, but their parents do also. The jargon used, for example at a meeting at children's services, must be understandable to the audience. I find myself in meetings thinking this case is going poorly for the parents because they do not understand what is being said to them. There are those who say that is just an excuse, but judging by the fact that I get calls after meetings from the parents and am asked the simplest of questions, I believe their confusion is real. That's why I break down the content into normal language, without all the acronyms, to help all the parties understand better. I can almost see the light bulb turn on.

One day, I was at a counseling session with my eleven-year-old foster son Buck. The counselor asked him how he liked his medical home visit. Buck looked at me confused and irritated. I asked the counselor to clarify what he meant by medical home visit, and he said, "How did he like the doctor he saw yesterday at his checkup?" Who thinks of these things? Say what you mean and mean what you say.

PROVIDE OPPORTUNITIES

Bad behaviors often result from good children being put in bad situations. Most of the time, out-of-control emotions happen because the situation is unfamiliar to the child, they are not well prepared for what is to come, and don't know how to act. Obviously, children cannot be prepared for all of life's scenarios, but if they have many experiences to draw from, chances are they will be able to infer enough information from past situations to know essentially how to act in a new situation.

A child who grows up confined mostly to a hotel room has fewer life experiences and street smarts than a child growing up and getting out of the home every day to attend school or other programs. A mom of seven children told me she doesn't need car seats in her van because she never takes her children out of the apartment. The point is to get children out into their world (whatever that looks like for your family) to experience diverse social settings.

Children imitate what they are exposed to. If children see adults stealing, skimping on the honesty factor, ignoring values, and having little emotional control, they will behave the same way. Words definitely have an effect, but what children see and experience will also shape their behaviors.

Keep in mind that every home is a school. Therefore, we must be conscious of what we are teaching in our school. We each have the obligation to help children learn how to handle themselves, and this is done partly by providing meaningful, diverse opportunities to expand their worldviews of people, places, and things. For this reason, parents should present managing emotions to children in a positive light, emphasizing the importance of adaptability, resilience, and being well-rounded.

CHAPTER 8: SOCIAL SKILLS

There's a lot that goes into teaching children social skills! Active parents take the time to teach children when they are young, so these skills become second nature as they mature. Social appropriateness is important because this is where caring and concern *for* others as well as cooperation *with* others comes from. Knowing how to correctly read and respond to social cues is a gift that keeps giving.

TRANSITIONS

Calmly transitioning between activities is one skill I spend a lot of time teaching. Having inadequate social skills weighs especially heavily on children's ability to transition from one activity to another.

On occasion, I meet a child who is well adjusted and can change activities seamlessly, but more often I am parenting children who are challenged with transitions. Many of my foster-mom peers and I notice that some children are a bundle of nerves with transitions and others can effortlessly change from one activity to another. Children who cannot progress through the order of daily events, without a major meltdown, can be exhausting to care for.

Our experiences with children range from simply lacking social exposure outside their home to caring for children who have spent extensive periods of time in a confined space. These circumstances affect how well the child sees the happenings around them and gives them clues about how to have socially acceptable responses. Sometimes the hesitation and fear about trying new things is compounded by a lack of understanding and communication. In the severe abuse and neglect cases, the children can be terribly upset with change and have a hard time warming up to any new experiences, much less knowing how to maneuver easy transitions.

Six-year-old Vince was afraid to go to school one Monday. He was overly hesitant and nervous, and I was having a hard time figuring out why. When he arrived home that afternoon, he told me with great relief that he did not have to go to Iowa after all for his "special testing" that day. Poor child thought that the Iowa Basic Tests we had been talking about meant he was leaving home to go to Iowa by himself for two weeks! That was a good lesson for me about every child reading situations differently and about communicating clearly.

Decoding fears and teaching coping skills regarding transitions takes time, but in the end this important skill helps the child connect better with others throughout their lifetime.

Children suffering with more severe communication issues will need gestures, smiles, pictures, or props to help them transition from task to task. A picture of their boots and coat will help them process that it is time to go outside. A pillow will prompt them to lie down for sleep. Packing a diaper bag or bookbag is also a signal to a child that school or an outing is approaching. We talk to the children as much as possible to prepare them for the next transition ahead.

Most, but not all, traumatized children being displaced from what is familiar to them are disconnected, confused, and scared and are just trying to survive. Teenager Kaye, whose teacher told me she constantly stood at the back of the room, expressed to the teacher that she felt anxious about joining in. Transitioning between classes and teachers made her anxious, so in order to cope, she took to observing from a distance. Compromising, her teachers agreed to allow a minute or two of pacing, as a way of calming herself in the back of the room, before she was expected to sit down and get to work.

Likewise, standoffishness can be an insecurity signal. Shiloh, fourteen, was a hands-off, curt, and distant child. She had a big chip on her shoulder, but when she would allow her emotional guard down, she was just a bundle of insecurity. She loved to do things over and over and may actually have been on the upper end of the autism spectrum, in my opinion.

She would string beads, sew, or craft with great intensity using repetitive motions until she felt herself becoming more comfortable enough to start whatever transition activity was being asked of her. Many times, the crafting activities had to be packed up to take in the car. We stopped short of letting her take them into events with her though because we felt she needed to be able to connect with others socially to decrease the degree of peer isolation she already felt.

Children who have not received early intervention for developmental delays like being deaf or mute can also have an extremely difficult time with transitions. One set of siblings that we watched for several respite time periods was deaf and essentially mute too. They were busy, chaotic, and very, very LOUD children. They had been placed in a foster home whose foster parents were dutifully tending to their many medical needs, but with three of them there were a lot of problems to address. We watched the children from time to time and witnessed the children become more engaged as medical support services were initiated. Hearing aids were obtained, language therapy was started, and spots at a special school for the hearing impaired opened up. I can't say that smooth transitions from one activity to another were ever a strong point for this trio, but given the level of adversity they faced daily it was easy to understand why getting their medical needs met eventually translated to better social behaviors overall.

When dealing with a child of typical development, we announce that a transition between activities is about to occur.

We try to orchestrate smooth transitions for children by briefly stating the time frame in ways they can understand. For younger children we might say, "You may go down the slide three more times before we sit down for lunch." To explain the church timeline, we prepare the children with, "We will be there the time it takes to watch two superhero episodes." We inform teens ahead of time of the family commitment so they have time to process what is being said and to close out what they are doing. I will tell the teens, "In fifteen minutes, I am leaving for the grocery store. If you're ready you can go along."

Some children process transitions very slowly. Sometimes, the only thing that helps as a parent is to remember that when children get loud and upset, you say a little prayer, stay calm, and be quiet. Then at least you know that one of you stayed in control. Once children get used to maintaining an order to our day, we can be less specific about timelines and move on with our day more quickly.

DIGGING THEIR HEELS IN

Obstinance is another type of behavior that parents get to address. We have seen unwillingness to compromise go one of two ways. Some children display low energy and refuse to participate, intending to punish those around them. Other times the obstinate behavior is full-blown negativity and aggression. Some doctors will treat this with medications if they suspect a true medical condition like depression or a conduct disorder, but most will not. Either way, the parent must find a way to live with it.

I feel bad for the child who is experiencing the need to choose obstinate behavior over cooperation. We try to read cues from the child or teen and head off full-scale conflicts, if we can, by curbing the stressors that are triggering them. We avoid physical altercations at all costs and always make sure the escape route is behind us if tensions are high, to ensure we have an open route to safety if needed. Downplaying these negative incidents as much as possible and persisting with family togetherness is the best way to realistically handle this. Burying themselves in media distraction to tune out the family would be discouraged, and beneficial coping mechanisms would be suggested instead. In reality, what we can control is to help them feel like they belong to something bigger than themselves.

Cheyenne was moody, but all the moods were a mix between being downtrodden, arrogant, and rude. She was hard to parent, so I have to say when we were asked to take an additional sibling group of teens in, we were unsure. Surprisingly, having the additional siblings join our family at the same time actually helped. They had many emotions that were up and down too, so we just carried on our normal level of activity around all the sulking individuals at once. With all the personalities in close quarters, we did not have time to dwell on one teen too much. Life was happening with everyone else around them. We chose to downplay the negative attitude and accentuate any hints of positivity. Aiming to be patient, giving them space when they needed it, and readily accepting them when they were ready to rejoin the group summed up our days.

We have limited technology time and downplay the importance of social media because it does not often support family values or good self-esteem. Our world of tech has a lot to do with intentional separation of the child from the family. We want our teens to enjoy their alone time but never to the extent of pushing adults away entirely. The more we allow our teens to hide out and be alone, the more reclusive they become. Pre-teens and teens may deny wanting to be involved with the family, but I think deep down staying connected with family bonding time is exactly what they want.

I prioritize touching base with each of my biological children almost daily, even though they are adults. I usually pick one or two foster teens to check in with too, on a rotational basis. In the spirit of teamwork, they are great about checking in with me also. Bonding is all about love and trust and support; no child is too old for that!

Conversely, my head knows that there are all sorts of reasons children shut others out. The focus on my heart is to pass along how to realistically survive life with children who display especially tough behaviors. Counselors and doctors see a teen for an hour and then send the parent home with the child and expect you to survive until their next appointment a week away. These are ideas about how to realistically outlast these behaviors outside that one-hour counseling session and prevent the children from reaching a point of stubbornness that is harder to come back from.

BELT-LOOP TIME

One parenting technique we like to use is called "belt-loop time." This idea started years ago when one of our little boys frequently needed close monitoring because of his violent outbursts. We needed a lot of energy to watch LaMont along with several other small children placed with us, and we were becoming overwhelmed with this constantly heightened care.

One day, we were swimming at my family reunion when, even after being asked to stop, LaMont would not stop dunking the other children. When he continued, I had him climb out of the water and hold onto the belt loop of my jeans while I chatted with my cousins. It was a sort of impromptu time-out station. After a few moments I asked LaMont if he would like to try swimming again with his new friends. He knew if he made a poor choice again, he would be back standing next to me for a longer period of time. He was able to return to the other children and the fun continued.

We originally thought belt-loop time was just an interruption of our foster son's behavior, but like many other surprises in foster care, over time this closeness to me became more of a calming activity for him. LaMont sometimes chose to grab my belt loop on his own, looking up at me as he felt that he was starting to get frustrated and needed a moment of my attention. Either way, he calmed down, and I could give him a moment of love and still concentrate on what I was doing. He would always receive a "good thinking" comment and a smile from me for choosing to curb his behaviors independently.

We mention this parenting technique because we want to be generous with praise while promoting safety and self-control. Sharing ideas and communicating the same rules with other adults who participate in the care of the child helps with continuity of expectations and better results. We want to be creative and kind in helping the child feel good about being in control of themselves and staying out of unnecessary mischief.

In addition, it is also necessary to modify what we do if we sense an uneasiness with a child in our care. If we see looks of insecurity or worry from the child, we stop to find out what's going on. In four-year-old Andie's case, she was afraid to sit on the steps alone as a time-out station because "it's too far away from you." We found out from her brother later that she had been left alone frequently during the daytime when their mom went to work and he went to school. The belt-loop idea worked better for her because she still experienced an interruption in her behavior and it gave her a break to calm herself, but being close to me seemed to make her less nervous.

PREVENTING STEALING

For varying reasons, some children tend to steal. Even though to most it is socially unacceptable, learning to think before understanding the significance of their actions takes a really long while to sink in, especially in traumatized children. We must keep a close eye on any child with stealing tendencies.

I have learned to glance in my foster children's pockets before completing the final payment at a store. Some don't think twice about stealing, and I want to discourage that behavior as soon as I discover it. If they do steal something, I have them return it immediately to the cashier, and I help them with a three-part apology, which includes addressing the person by name, stating what they did, and offering an apology. For example, "I'm sorry, Miss Cashier, that I stole your candy bar. I need to give it back to you." Simply putting it back on the shelf without owning up to the stealing would be a missed learning opportunity for the child to understand desired social skills.

Donte (four) had such a kind heart toward others and wanted to help us whenever he had the chance. He grew up exposed to a mother with a stealing problem and was often recruited by her to assist. One day, he heard me comment admiringly about a beautiful Christmas wreath hanging from our neighbor's garage. Sweet thing, he said for me to wait till after dark and then he and his mama would get it for me. I had to explain to him that while I appreciated the sentiment, we are not allowed to steal just because we want something.

Hadley and Heather had a serious stealing incident while living in our home. Hadley asked me one day, completely out of the blue, if she and her sister could get a cell phone with their own money. They showed me a crisp $50 bill that supposedly first came from chore money that they saved from "way before" they were in foster care. Then the story changed, and they said the money came from their father when they entered foster care and who had supposedly handed it to them as they rushed out the door. Finally, the story shifted to finding the money at the visitation center behind the trash can in the bathroon. We were fairly sure none of these stories was true.

Ron arranged for the four of us to meet with the local sheriff and his female detective to have a friendly discussion about being careful about the choices they make in life and how choices now will affect their future. They continued to lie to the police officers throughout the meeting, but after a few days, guilt set in enough for Heather to admit that she had stolen it from the kitchen counter of one of our alternative caregivers on a weekend respite. Her rationale was that she never had money before and wanted it. Heather gave the money back to our alternative caregiver, apologized verbally and by letter to both the caregiver and the police officers, and they both spent a day at the respite home doing yard chores to rectify the crime. We did our best to show them the consequences of their actions.

Older children can think that life is unfair, so they feel justified with their stealing. They often factor in a family connection to the act, such as their mom says that stealing is not really that big of a deal. They may feel bonded or loyal to their parents or friends by doing it. We try to show them that this falsehood allows them to lie to themselves that wrong is right.

We parents may be the only "Jesus example" that children experience. It's important to call the children on the negative action and teach them why it matters to work for what they want instead of stealing. There are a lot of conflicting messages in our society about this, so the children might see and hear mixed messages. We have to try to at least plant those seeds in the hopes that children will remove stealing from how they want to live.

SILLY GIRL STUFF

Peer gossiping drama and other minor incidents that tend to be especially strong in girls is a social phenomenon we refer to in our home as "silly girl stuff." Though we do see this with boys, they do not seem to let hurtful comments linger as long as girls do. We ignore this behavior and teach socially appropriate responses to girls' gossiping. While listening to an occasional concern is reasonable, dwelling on constant negativity takes an emotional toll on all the participants in the home, including Mom and Dad. As a result, we do not waste much time on minor silly girl stuff drama because it is counterproductive to all the positive social skills we are working to emphasize.

Instead, our suggestion to the endless stream of "friend worries" is to tell the children to say a little prayer for the drama-producing child and ignore the behavior, if possible. We also ask them if they have ever heard of the saying *Talk less, say more*. If they can learn to stay out of the drama altogether, they will demonstrate to their friends that they do not need to gossip to have fun and therefore will not be drawn into those conversations as often.

If that does not satisfy them, then we ask, "What can you do to change the situation?" emphasizing that we cannot change how someone else feels or thinks, we can only control ourselves. We explain that our control is limited to deciding if we want to be coerced into saying or doing something we feel uncomfortable about. Our advice generally centers around sticking with what you believe to be kind, leaving the area, and getting busy finding a new activity to participate in.

Our eight-year-old foster daughter Kym was absolutely outstanding at ignoring silly girl stuff. Not only did her three sisters like to instigate silly girl issues in our home, which she did a great job staying out of, but she also came from a classroom where her teacher was apparently not attentive to the feelings of a certain classmate, Shaun'te. Kym would tell us about trying to play with Shaun'te on the playground by offering to be her friend when no one else would. She said she did not think Shaun'te knew how to be nice to others and so she wanted to "teach her." Shaun'te was still not very nice in return, and Kym took teasing from the other girls about it, but she had a truly kind heart and would go into school every morning with the attitude that she wanted to remain cheerful and determined in her desires to include Shaun'te anyway. We were proud of her attempts to manage this second-grade silly girl stuff drama on her own and complimented her attempted kindness.

THE BULLY

Sometimes silly girl stuff advances to bullying. Bullying behavior is tough because first we need to protect the target of the bully, but then we also must help the child understand *why* someone bullies. First, I want to address what we have learned about bullies through our years of parenting. Bullies are missing key social skills. This usually comes from trauma they themselves have suffered, so they use the "toughness" to cover the hurt. Feeling important and being in control is what most bullies thrive on. I know it is hard to think about the bully's personal issues when emotions are high, but the longer I take care of children, the more I see it as an immensely important factor to understand.

In my experience, bullying starts with targeting the victim's self-esteem. The recipient of the bullying feels powerless to call out the bully's meanness fearing the situation will get worse. While bullying behaviors cannot be justified, I stress considering why they are doing what they are doing. By understanding what their deficits are and what is missing from their support system, we can sometimes diffuse the situation. The more experience I gain, the more clearly I can see that childhood trauma makes bullies. The bullies we know come from broken homes with little parental supervision.

Bullies have passed through my home on occasion, which means I have been thrust into the role of parenting a bully. It is an interesting place to sit. One foster child Lia was a kindergartener, and the terrible actions she came up with were astounding. She would steal, hit, kick, or punch anyone annoying her, easily taking out her peers on the playground.

The final straw came when she spit in the bus driver's face while being reprimanded and got thrown off the bus. With the need to now be driven to school, she missed spending any time with the only child she did like who was a student at another elementary school in town and who only rode the one neighborhood bus route together. Her lack of social skills resulted in a loss of time with her little friend. On our rides to school, we talked through how to be a good friend on the playground to develop appropriate social skills. After interacting with her biological father on several occasions, I could see that she did what she did to survive his rough parenting style. It helped me better understand why she acted in the bully-like way she did.

One pack of little brothers was the same way. They all had bullying behaviors. I understand that boys can be rough and tumble, but this was different; they flat-out and mercilessly bullied each other and any other child around them. Their go-to actions included hair pulling, punching, digging fingernails, pulling arms and legs hard, twisting heads, purposefully breaking things, hurling items across the room, verbal put-downs, and lots of cursing. They ganged up on each other, and it was within their mantra for three brothers to beat on one brother the minute my back was turned. We tried to control their bullying, but with five of them it was maintenance at best. Again, after I met the boys' parents, the boys seemed like little helpless pups in comparison to the adults. They learned in their family that it was socially acceptable, and dare I say seemed encouraged, for the older sibling to beat on the younger ones to put them in their place. One brother said to me, "I allowed to beat him, I older."

On the flip side, there are silent bullies where subtle gestures and comments are meant to insult another. This happens especially when teens blame their persistent negativity on just having fun or playing around. This is probably not true. When teens or adults do not know how to interact with others politely in society, they are isolated and excluded. Essentially, this makes matters worse because they are often hard children to love. What they really need are extra layers of love and more adult attention from parent figures to help them heal from their own traumas and loneliness. Obviously, this is a big job for our current society.

When a younger child has bullying behaviors, we separate the bully child's play area from the target child and insist upon separate activities until they can respect the other. They are kept especially busy until they can play cooperatively. Circumstances can be that they don't get much of a break from each other because they go to school together and then they come home to play together, as in the case of siblings or foster children.

One such example in our home was a set of preteen girls who were not related. The dominant child (Avery) would slyly pick a game or activity to play that she was superior in with the more socially awkward peer (Cheyenne), so she would always win. Avery was passive aggressive in her play, drawing Cheyenne in because she was lonely and wanted desperately to be accepted. Unfortunately, this always ended up in tears of frustration for Cheyenne because she routinely lost, and Avery was not a gracious winner. After this happened a few too many times, we switched the provided after-school activities to noncompetitive ones like arts and craft projects and puzzles. Eventually, Cheyenne found a friend at school who invited her to a youth group at her church. This helped with her sense of belonging and filled that need for friendship. Having these two girls participate in separate activities helped ease tensions too.

We have found the best medicine for the escalating bully, if they are living in our house, is intense parent involvement. The bully is kept especially close by and busy. Media is monitored because much of what children know about bullying comes from what they see and hear online. We offer a variety of activities in our home so the desire for social media is limited. There are times that bullying comes from boredom and boredom comes from too much time thinking about one's own woes. This in turn increases the child's vulnerability to be sucked into more negativity in the media. It's a bad cycle. Dedication, patience, and grit are needed to parent the bully. I think there is value in finding some form of volunteer work for them also.

Parenting children other than your own is especially difficult since you have no control over how the other parents are raising them when they are away from you. We adjust. We try to teach empathy, kindness, and compassion, and we strongly discourage physical violence even though witnessing routine domestic violence is a norm for some children. We start with modeling the behavior that is expected from each of our family members, and we spend a lot of active time together. Every day of parenting a bully will call for extra energy and dedication to help them heal from their traumas, grow in their social skills, and find momentum to achieve kinder peer interactions.

THE TARGET

The victim is the ever-important person being targeted by the bully. We want to listen to children's concerns and do what is in our control to help. Most times, children do not need us to solve their problems for them but to be a caring soundboard to bounce ideas off of. I often think of the man who carried the cross for Jesus. He did not prevent Jesus' suffering, but he walked beside him and carried the weight of the load as he could. That is how we look at supporting the victims of bullying.

Some coping skills we talk with our teens about include saying yes to a bully but in a safe way. We had Cheyenne tell Avery, "I want to do something fun with you, but I do not want to play board games. Let's ask if we can use our gift cards today to go and get pizzas for dinner." Cheyenne had also been given permission to blame Ron and me when dealing with Avery's pushiness. She could say, "No way, I can't play a mean trick on the little kids! Miss K and Mr. Ron just got done talking to me about that last night!" We step in to guide the situation when needed.

We also feel that it is helpful to ask an emotionally frail child what helps them feel safe. We listen to their ideas and follow through when we can. Cheyenne liked the door chimes to know when someone was coming and going. Avery preferred sleeping in a room surrounded by only her sisters. So, we installed magnetic door chimes on their doors, that way if an issue warranted us needing to be awakened at night we would be alerted. Avery and Cheyenne did sleep in separate rooms with well-informed bunkmates who knew what was going on. Between the chimes and others' knowledge, we felt we had a good handle on the girls' safety.

We do believe in counseling for teens, especially if a good match with a therapist can be found. We also think of providing opportunities for volunteering, music, art, sports, or library clubs as options to create a pleasant experience for children. Spending time at the YMCA pool was a big fallback for stressful days the year we had Avery and Cheyenne in our home. We have also been known to enroll a child in karate class because physical activity and having useful skills build confidence. We encourage children to have a relationship with God and to pray for guidance, patience, and kindness. Layering the weaker child with kindness from the heart in any way that is under our control is the goal.

If bullies can be identified and helped earlier on, the incidents of escalating antisocial behaviors throughout their lifetime can be decreased, therefore decreasing their need to control others. This is why parents raising kind children in every home matters. We also encourage the target child to not let the endless victimhood role creep into their thinking. It is a chapter in time that usually passes, and it does not get to define the child forever. Resiliency is a superpower. We stress that. Those who can show empathy toward others, embrace differences, and show tolerance can make our families, communities, and society stronger.

NO-THANK-YOU LIST

We have found that building good manners in children is an important aspect of developing their social skills. To help them avoid awkward personal situations, we allow all our children a "no-thank-you list." This is a short list of a few items that they do not want to eat or do. The goal is to make life easier on all members of the family and decrease trauma, whining, and complaining. We try hard to honor these requests and to make their voices heard. We find that this list gives children an opportunity to practice their manners by exercising "yes please" and "no-thank-you" responses when offered a choice by an adult.

Six-year-old Katie strongly disliked all soups and never wanted it near her. Apparently, her family ate canned soup almost every day when food was available at her home. She seemed to associate soup with unpleasant times. This sweet girl chose five flavors of soup for her list to ensure that none would ever be served to her, even though I assured her that "soup" was enough to cover all varieties. She was still offered all foods when we served a meal, but she was taught proper etiquette and declined politely with a learned "no thank you, Miss K" response, especially with soup.

Tre did not have the focus to clean and organize toys. He wound up playing instead and then became frustrated that he never seemed to be finished with the job. Though he was not permitted to purposefully make large messes for others to clean, he was allowed to add toy organizing projects to his no-thank-you list. Thankfully, he liked to use the sweeper. His sister Gabby felt the opposite, as she was a master toy organizer but never ever wanted to sweep. We all have our gifts.

Eight-year-old Kelly had a strong aversion to any green vegetables. She went so far as to gag and choke on them on purpose. This type of upset is not one to fool with because dieticians have explained to us that this strong reaction can lead to the start of an eating disorder. We explained to Kelly that gagging and choking were not good manners for the dinner table but that she could simply say "no thank you" instead. We compromised with Kelly that no broccoli or spinach would be served, but she agreed she could manage green beans and salads with dressing.

Down the road, we decided to nonchalantly put a few carrots and celery sticks out on the counter while Kelly was anxiously waiting for the meal preparations to be completed. She was hungry from her day and decided "maybe" she could try a few bites. She decided our vegetables tasted fresh, cold, and crunchy and soon became accustomed to having this special pre-meal snack, which we were all surprised she liked. When she finally went home, her dad was pleased with this idea and said it worked well for him too. We use every opportunity to teach, no matter how small the lesson.

We had six siblings one time who appreciated not being forced to eat a one-size-fits-all meal. They all had different tastes. Two loved stew of any kind, two leaned vegetarian, and two were my all-things strawberry girls. Coming from the Caribbean Islands, they all shared a cultural love for seafood. We always honored their individual no-thank-you lists and gladly provided their favorite treat of sushi for every birthday meal request. These are reasonable requests that I am willing to allow the children to control. Small concessions such as a no-thank-you list teach compromise and negotiation, important social skills, and allow for compassion for the child.

BE HAPPY

Another technique we use to help keep our home running smoothly is the suggestion of happiness. This spans letting our children know everything we are happy to do for them *as well as* everything we are happy to wait for. I say, "I'm happy to get snacks out as soon as the toys are put away" or "I'm happy to get peanut butter cereal at the store after the fruity ones you picked last week are eaten."

Kaye was often found awake late at night. My response to her would be something like, "I'm happy for you to journal past bedtime. Remember we leave for church at 7:45 am tomorrow." Her late-night writing habits were brought to her attention as well as the unspoken expectation for her to be cheerfully prompt and ready to leave on time for church.

We also combine the happiness technique with the brain drain technique, when needed. Fifteen-year-old Rob was a likable young man; however, his favorite delay tactic was his gift of charm, smiling, and stalling. "I am happy to drive you to soccer practice as soon as the computer area is tidied" was my response to him wanting to head out the door. Every argumentative statement that the mess will all be gotten out again when he got home may have been true, but I would not go back on my original request. To keep our home under control, we tidy up our area when we leave the house. I would answer back with the same single calm response about what I am happy to do for him: "I am happy to drive you to soccer practice as soon as the computer area is tidied." I let the shame of arriving late to practice and running laps up and down the bleachers, as required by the coach, be the punishment as I drove away from the parking lot unscathed. The area was tidied, the teenage brain drain did not force me into nagging, and I was happy as our foster son was busy for the next three hours under his coach's watchfulness.

Another take on the be happy technique is modeling how to genuinely be happy for other persons' successes. This is such a huge lesson to teach all children, as they benefit from learning to be sincere about others' accomplishments. We teach children that learning to be happy for another person will help bring positive energy back to themselves. Our local ballet teacher demonstrated this idea to us years ago by complimenting her dancers. In class, when she saw a nice improvement in a dancer's skill, she stopped the class briefly, had the dancer showcase their new skill, and asked all the dancers to clap for the child being momentarily featured. As the dancers aged, they were automatic in their encouraging responses when a peer's ability was recognized. We thought this was such a simple and effective way to build a child up and adjusted the details to fit our home.

Since we share some of our own disappointments with our children, we also want to make time to share our joy. Our general rule of thumb is for every correction or criticism we point out, we attempt to follow it with two comments regarding some form of pleasantry or happiness. They may not be specifically about the child and may just be an observation, such as, "The sun coming out today was a nice surprise, and I'm glad we got to go to the lake to swim." Or "I was happy with the behavior at the lake today. Everyone was helpful at clean-up time. Who wants to tell Mr. Ron about our day?" I make a point to acknowledge and talk about happiness in our daily report. Sometimes having a pleasant and joyful disposition is about talking yourself into it. Martha Washington once said, "The greater part of our happiness or misery depends on our dispositions and not on our circumstances."

Encouraging children to take over the thoughts they let into their mind makes for a happier tomorrow. I remind children and teens that they are not the only ones who are tempted with things we should not do or think. It takes maturity, self-discipline, and a desire to choose what is right, not what is easy, to achieve true happiness. Choosing the straight and narrow path will have its rewards later.

WORK ETHIC

The next social skill we emphasize is having a strong work ethic. We explain to children that a strong work ethic, when practiced, becomes a way of life, whether that is how to be studious in school or how to stay employed. Simply being on time and putting in a good effort are characteristics that are deeply appreciated in the workforce. Working toward having a goal in life with learned skills allows us to then earn money. We use that paycheck to buy items from others, which supports their business and their livelihood. If we are able bodied, we don't want to solely rely on others for long-term support, becoming dependent for our livelihood.

As foster parents, Ron and I see this every day as we are pulled back and forth between a world of independently caring for ourselves and one with families supported heavily by a government-funded system. My hope is that, by explaining this concept, others can understand how much children are intrigued by the idea of choosing a path that controls their own destiny—once they know about it. Many people mistakenly think children in foster care and their families want to be dependent on others their whole lives, but many have told us they would like nothing better than to be able to provide for themselves.

As a teen, Rose's only life experience with food and housing was the food stamps and government housing vouchers her mother received. She wanted to know why we did not use these programs and asked, "Why do you pay for your own groceries?" We shared that assistance programs help in the short term but that people who have the ability should work for their living and provide for their own needs. She had no idea about any of this. Being an intelligent girl, she was intrigued. She thought everyone lived the way she and her family did.

She instigated many conversations around this topic of work ethic and providing for herself in the future. She went on to share that she always wanted to fly a plane. Further conversations got her interested in the military. By the time she left our house a year later, she asked me if we would put a "My daughter is in the Army" sign in our yard if she made it. We told her of course! That would make us proud! She had not experienced working parents before or understood the importance of working consistently, pursuing natural abilities, and searching out career choices until she came into foster care. We strongly support developing children's talents and gifts that will carry them into the future.

BONDING

Well-bonded children make for stronger family ties and more stable societies. Aim for bonding moments when parenting your child. I say moments because when we parent young children it is easy to spend endless time with them making memories every day, but as our children age and become independent the idea of still needing to keep them connected and bonded to the family is realistically found in everyday moments here and there.

Secure attachments form the basis of all future relationships, a sense of self-worth, resilience to stress, the ability to regulate emotions, and they create meaningful connections with others.[6] Bonding makes it easier to process thoughts and cope with life's surprises. Having a strong emotional bond with a parent figure promotes stability and socially accepted behaviors. At any age, bonding decreases chaos and helps the child feel grounded and connected. Many people have heard the adage, "I could never be a foster parent because I could never give the children up." Our hearts *are* sad when children leave, but think about it this way instead: Bonding is the whole point! All bonds, with responsible figures, are good. New bonds do not erase old ones. We are careful to support both.

If there is another family in the child's life, they should not be taboo. No matter what kind of parenting circumstance you and your child are in, it is not the child's fault. We encourage children to show their feelings for both families when there is more than one involved. We want them to remain bonded. Having photos of the child's biological family on the fridge or running through digital frames are ways to preserve the children's past, offer comfort, and make it okay for them to love and talk openly about their family. It is desirable for children to be encouraged to have affection with their "new" family and stay bonded to their own family as well.

Some children have come from rough homes, and it is not always easy to support the other family, especially when abuse or neglect has occurred. Children can absolutely sense the feelings toward the other family, and it can make them feel torn because children typically still love their mom and dad deeply despite any maltreatment. We can always do our job to protect the children, but being the judge and jury toward another doesn't typically bode well, is draining emotionally, and the child can suffer when sensing the animosity. May I humbly suggest that we be as kind to everyone as is humanly possible and let God sort the rest out later? Even if the kindness is not reciprocated, you will come out the hero in the end to the children because you respected their family.

Instead, I will attempt to help the struggling family by teaching them about trauma-parenting ideas, good bonding, and why parents' actions have such a lasting effect on their children and their psyche. When you come up with a clever parenting idea that is working for a particular child, share your knowledge and experience in an attempt to keep the expectations similar for the child trying to manage their behaviors.

I do not support any attempts to replace the child's original family. I think in most cases being truthful about their situations is best as I've seen deception fail too many times. I can think of at least six of our foster sons, just off the top of my head, who do not get to see their fathers because they are incarcerated. Three of the boys are faring better with this information and can talk about their dads, know what the crime committed was, and know where their dads are geographically. They each have a relative who keeps up to date with the dads. Even though, to my knowledge, none of the boys goes to the prisons to visit, they seem to have a relatively healthy understanding of the situation and bond with their dad.

The other three boys do not know about their dads' history. They are aware that they are in jail, but all the other details have been kept from them. They seem to place these dads on mental pedestals and fantasize excessively on their innocence and victimhood, which is not as healthy of an outlook. I anticipate that as these boys grow into adulthood the three boys who had a distant but true knowledge of their dads will be better prepared to meet up with them one day as opposed to the three who do not.

I never met a child who suffered from too much love, and I am a strong believer that children cannot have too many adults who care about them. I help my children realize that they are fortunate to have so many people who love them. Our alumni teen foster daughter Nadia tells the little ones she comes over to help me with, "I'm lucky, I have three moms . . . my birth mom, my foster mom, and my mommy mom [her adoptive mom]!" She certainly is a well-bonded and well-loved child.

Parents who have put the time into teaching social skills have children who feel confident in their own abilities and who know stability. Stability affects their maturity and their readiness to understand and process the rules of the world around them.

CHAPTER 9: SEIZE THE DAY

Many of us find that having a consistent schedule and approach to life helps keep our brains focused and knowing what to expect. Children also need this same mindset and to be given the opportunity to have some say over their days' schedules and happenings. Having routine and structure will translate to extra minutes of peace in your day.

ROUTINES

Children who experience daily routines respond better behaviorally because they know what is expected of them. We have fostered many infants and know that even with babies this is true. One summer day, the mother of our two young foster children gave birth to twin siblings. Thankfully, the premature babies were only one month early so they were fairly stable medically. As soon as the infants came home to us from the hospital, we set a routine of feeding, naps, tummy time, and rocking time with music and playing in their swings. The afternoon schedule was similar.

During the third rotation in the evening time, we added a bath before bed. The babies started to thrive immediately, as evidenced by small developmental steps like good head control, tracking moving objects with their eyes, and steady weight gain. Experienced parents know that routine activities done at the same time, for the same interval, in the same order, bring comfort to the very young. Later that year when the four were adopted, they were so accustomed to our routines that the adoptive parents said this alone greatly eased the transition on all of them.

Steady routines also make school-aged children more comfortable with what is going on around them, especially since they typically do not have a lot of say in the events of the day. The unknown can cause trepidation, but stability leads to confidence, and confidence leads to well-thought-out behavior choices.

Five-year-old Drue attended only a handful of classes the year he was supposed to be in kindergarten because it was not a high priority for his mother. By the time he was brought into foster care due to neglect, it was already the winter term. Because he had not been taught at home or gone to any preschool or Head Start programs, he was far behind his peers academically and behaviorally. His behaviors were extreme, as evidenced by his argumentative and confrontational nature. He had difficulty regulating his emotions; these outbursts were daily occurrences that we and the school staff had to learn to tame. Thank goodness for his very patient and amazing teachers! Once he started attending regularly, he wanted to go to school so badly every day to be with friends and teachers, have a steady routine, and learn. He would actually cry after school because he did not want to leave at the end of the day. What a change we saw in Drue!

Teens need routines too, albeit less structured. Going to school regularly builds relationships, healthy habits, and increases children's knowledge and accountability. When teens are truant from school, they typically do not have a steady routine in their life. This could result in many areas of disorganization, like being unprepared for the day and not completing school assignments. This lack of routine makes it worse because they are easily frustrated due to being so far behind their peers in their studies. The idea of getting into a routine by going to school EVERY day, even when they have a headache, feel fatigued, or are doctoring a split nail must be overcome.

Eventually, our older foster children learn that the school routine will not change based on their daily grievances. Relationships with teachers and friends start to improve because they are consistently present each day. Though they may not admit it, once teens get used to the idea, most find comfort in the social and educational aspects of having steady meals, friends, and something new to learn. They discover that after-school time can now be filled with changing extracurricular activities of their choosing.

Besides schooling, some children need other rudimentary aspects of their lives to be overseen also. Quite surprisingly, some of the simplest of routines like eating, bathing, and changing clothes regularly must be specified. These hygiene basics are a very important routine that might seem straightforward to most but are foreign to some.

Buck said he and his brother rarely wore underwear under their jeans because their mom would give their briefs away to the men who regularly passed through their home. They were surprised to have clean clothes provided to them after they showered that first night. I actually had to have them go back to the bathroom and put the clean outfits on because, to my astonishment, they came out of the bathroom wearing the same dirty clothes they were wearing before the shower. Buck said, "I want to save those clean clothes for tomorrow." I had to explain that getting into bed with dirty clothes would dirty his bed linens and that we would provide clean clothes again in the morning. This led to a follow-up conversation about what bed linens were. Sigh, it was a lot for the late hour of 3 am.

Getting into a routine is the perfect time to give church a try. Starting every week off with the guidance and positivity of a church service on Sunday sets the routine for the whole week. We are matter of fact about going to church, and while children in foster care can refuse to go, we encourage them to give it a chance and most of the time they do!

Theo was the only fella that I can recall who did not want to go to church. However, during the post-church brunch at home, he always asked us questions about the morning. There was clearly still interest there. It's a good idea to think about faith like this: Friends, homes, and schools may change, but having a relationship with Jesus and the camaraderie that having a church routine provides do not. Having God to rely on is greatly beneficial to some of the loneliest people I have ever been involved with.

BEDTIME

Sleep training is one of the more difficult aspects of parenting but can be cured with redirection, consistency, and follow-through. Bedtime problems occur for reasons such as lack of a consistent bedtime; lacking an appropriate place to sleep; technology in the bedroom; or being hungry, cold, or scared. We tend to these needs first before beginning sleep training. At any age, being able to keep to a consistent bedtime schedule obviously is best for children but is not always convenient for the parent, which reveals the real problem.

Parents who believe in active parenting know that they themselves cannot stay up excessively late every night because they need to be fresh in the morning to engage with their children. Children in foster care often come from an environment where lack of structure is common because of substance abuse issues and/or the parents wanting their children to sleep in as late as possible in the morning. They may stick their children in front of the TV or other electronics because they do not want to be disturbed when sleeping in late.

We have had foster children with odd sleep routines that have come about because their parents were participating in late-night adult activities and took the children along with them. The late-night activity of choice for Jade and Claire's family was drug sales. Louisa's family was prostitution. Destiny and Dustie told us they were routinely forced to watch horror movies with their dad late into the night.

To break these erratic nighttime habits, we choose to stick to a routine, keeping the bedtime schedule nearly the same seven days a week. At bedtime, when the phrase "time for closing ceremonies" is announced in our home, the children know to tidy their play area and come over and say goodnight. We make sure that we follow the same routine each night by going upstairs for bathroom time, donning pajamas, adjusting the lights, reading a book, and putting the music box on. Once the routine is completed, getting out of bed is discouraged unless there is a potty emergency or a fire (Oh, and I guess there was the night that tree fell on the house in a windstorm!).

One of our older foster sons who visits often has taken it upon himself to be the public service announcer that "closing ceremonies have begun" because he knows our routine so well. It brings a laugh from us all. He is a good example for the younger children and is becoming quite the leader! Part of our routine includes tucking in everyone—young and old—with goodnight wishes and hugs. We gently offer a suggestion to say a goodnight prayer for their family and something they are thankful for.

School-agers Bryant and Cara both had trouble adjusting to bedtime at our house. We spent quite a few nights getting them used to an age-appropriate evening routine. Eventually, the caseworker told us that their dad would let the children sleep with a TV on in their room all night long. We told Bryant that he was allowed to use a music box in his room at bedtime, but we do not have televisions in children's bedrooms. There were several nights of big crocodile tears from him, but we were finally successful in changing the bedtime protests around by keeping our requested routine constant. We would always reassure him that he didn't need to worry because his body would go to sleep when it needed to.

For parents who have allowed problematic bedtime refusals to develop, utilizing the brain drain and redirection techniques together will help to correct the problem. Once the child becomes familiar with the routine, condense the entire bedtime explanation request down to a single sentence. If the child chooses to get out of bed, we walk the child back to bed and calmly state the same one sentence.

One child, who I like to refer to as my little Houdini, springs to mind simply because she absolutely would not stay in bed. She could climb into, out of, and over anything. She had a never-ending list of reasons why she was out of bed and had the energy of ten children. My chosen sentence to her every night as I walked her back to bed and tucked her in countless times was "Good night sweetheart, have a good sleep." There was no hint of anger, and the tone of voice, volume, and words never changed. Eventually (fifteen returns to bed is my record), she got tired and fell asleep; the next night was easier because she knew I would not change my rules. Mercifully, now when she comes to visit, she is a great sleeper and a role model for other children in the house!

LET THEM SEE THE LIGHT

Extreme anxiety around darkness can be seen in many children. For some of the children who pass through our home and because of their past demons, one night-light at bedtime probably won't cut it. Rationalization does not help much either. What we have found to be helpful is allowing each child, even if they share a room, to have control over some kind of light in their area of the bedroom. They are permitted to use it as they see fit until they progress enough to feel comfortable with just the hall light on. If another child in the room does not like the light on, then they are offered a silk light-blocking eye mask to try, and we have found this extra pampering to be a big hit!

Drue wanted to sleep with all eight lights available in or near his room on. We gave him multiple night-lights to use rather than turning on the overhead lights. He resisted, though, and wanted his room to be as bright at night as it was during the day. Because eight lights were unreasonable and he would get up to turn them on anytime we turned a few of them off, we were forced to unscrew some of the bulbs to curb his anxiety and give him a dim area to sleep in. His fear was sure real.

As we took a walk one morning, I introduced him to an elderly neighbor who asked him where he was from, and he answered, "the dark hotel room." What a sad and revealing response that was. This helped me realize that Drue's anxiety at bedtime was much deeper than just fearing the dark.

OUR FRIEND THE CLOCK

Our son Matthew, as a teen, came up with the next parenting technique in response to wanting to teach his foster siblings at the time (ages eight to fourteen) about reading a clock and staying in bed past the crack of dawn on Saturdays. Since few of our foster children can tell the time on a clock face, we encourage the development of this skill by purposely not having digital clocks. Matthew drew a picture showing what 8:30am looked like so they knew what the position of the hands should match up to before they were allowed to begin being up and about for the day. His goal was meant to discourage noise from these seven girls and all their time primping in the bathroom so early in the morning on Saturdays—his only day to sleep in. The children easily slept to this time on school days but mysteriously didn't sleep in at all on the weekends. It's like this inner superpower sense they have. This idea worked without us having to police the clock, and the children had a few lessons in telling time. Having this last bit of sleep before the weekend starts in full blast mode helps with our longevity as a foster home. Sometimes it's the little things that count.

Again, this wake-up theory also has the added benefit of reinforcing how to tell time. Our set of four school-agers—Mike, Dustin, Frank, and Kyle—literally did not know how to sleep through the night. Since they didn't understand time well, we would frequently find them roaming the house and playing games or getting into mischief with each other in the middle of the night because they "thought it was time to be awake." After a couple of nights of practice going to bed at 9 pm, with the use of a picture schematic of the face of the clock, and knowing what time they could be up and about, the boys started learning how to sleep through the night at seven, eight, nine, and ten years old. As a hidden benefit, they began to enjoy reading more because this was considered an acceptable alternative for sleeplessness in the middle of the night or if they awakened early. This clock idea has been golden for us.

My foster-mom friend Patricia likes to use a bedtime pass as a reward in her home. If the child does a good job with their bedtime routine, stays in bed, and awakens at an appropriate time, they earn a bedtime pass that can be redeemed for various treats or ten extra minutes on the video games the following night. I haven't needed that idea myself yet, but it's on my radar for future placements.

One last trick we have been using for thirty years is to watch the New Year's ball drop using the replay of the Australia coverage. We jump up and down and use noise makers to bring in the New Year then get all the little ones off to bed shortly after 9 pm EST. Change around the details to what works best for your family, but these clock ideas have helped our sanity immensely.

SLEEP-IN SATURDAY

As I mentioned before, we have a tradition called sleep-in Saturday. Every Friday night at the beginning of our bedtime closing ceremonies, someone will remember to yell, "Remember it's sleep-in Saturday tomorrow!" Now don't get too excited. Our goal is for everyone to be quiet and in their beds for an extra half hour on Saturdays to allow those of us who like to sleep in a bit to do this one day a week. I bring this small luxury up because sleep deprivation is such a true stress in parenting. We all know that parents of young children face this challenge temporarily, but eventually most families outgrow this stage and settle into a sleep routine that works for their family. This is different with families who foster as a vocation because we are constantly welcoming new children, and all who enter must be taught sleep training all over again.

To increase our odds of a successful morning, we teach the children present in our home that Saturdays are a bit of a different circumstance from our Monday through Friday routine. We are clear about what is expected of them and that they may always get up to use the bathroom, but they must go back to their room to rest or read until 9:00am rolls around. If *everyone* makes it quietly to 9:00am without waking another family member up, that is a huge success!

Our home may function differently than a home with the same children day in and day out. Children with a consistent home life of course know their own home rules, but in our case, we frequently have different children present from one night to the next.

Friends Tre and Howard still visit and have sleepovers from time to time at our home, years after living here. As they giggle, they always remember to remind each other of the Sleep-In Saturday ritual as they head off to sleep on Friday night. We are grateful that we have mutual respect for each other, and the boys have no trouble being in their room quietly on Saturday mornings.

PREPARE FOR THE DAY

We tell children ahead of time where the errands of the day will take us. We have quick morning briefings to convey the chores and tasks that need to be accomplished before we start our day. We typically have also spoken about the day's agenda the night before when clothes were set out too.

On shopping days, making a list of locations we are headed to and sometimes allowing the children to add something to the list helps them feel more an active part of the process. The children will be less cranky as the day's activities start because of the proper preparation and anticipation. Politely informing, instead of catching the child off guard, threatening, and over-promising, is a more effective approach. Children sincerely appreciate being communicated with because they feel like their time is important too. Children do not want to feel dragged along. They want to feel worthwhile and included.

Drue, hailing from that abusive and neglectful background, grew up (for years!) in a tiny, dirty hotel room. He had anxieties beyond the darkness fears. Nearly every activity change upset him, and transitions were a nightmare because he was sure whatever lay ahead was not good. He also had no sense about coming back to whatever he was currently involved in as something he could start up again. Specifically, his past experiences had taught him that he never knew how long they would be in the same hotel before having to move again. It was a long while before we could calm his nervousness enough to understand what preparing for the day ahead entailed. Our saving grace was that he enjoyed having his own pictorial schedule of the day's events to carry around and look at.

Our three two-year-old little girls were delighted to each have a copy of the shopping list to carry along in the grocery cart with them as we started on a day of big box shopping. They learned a little bit about delayed gratification as they waited for the surprises each aisle held, were kept entertained with their special-colored pencil, and marked their lists as they saw fit, just like Foster Mom was doing. We were prepared for the day, the three little girls were kept busy, and we all enjoyed the outing.

CLEVER PACKING AND UNPACKING

Trying to get out the door when it comes to having children requires good organization. One necessary parenting technique is to build extra packing time into the day. We have strategies for the car, the medical equipment, and anything else we might need, all with designated packing and unpacking routines.

Stocking the car with various emergency supplies and stashing them in the car is the best way to be prepared for the unexpected. Planning ahead means our car supply includes a variety of diapers, underpants, deodorant, feminine supplies, wipes, and several pairs of black shorts and leggings in various sizes. We choose black stretchy items because they fit almost any-sized child, boys or girls, and match any colored shirt that is being worn at the time, which draws less attention to any mishaps. We have run to our car supply so many times throughout the years that we cannot count them. We have also shared our supplies with others in need.

Well-thought-out packing is especially helpful for children with medical needs as well as for families with multiple children. The diaper bag or overnight respite bag can be organized with separate gallon bags to help find items easily. Foster-friend Kris started us on this strategy years ago with her six adopted children all under the age of six. She saved time by organizing all the diapering supplies in labeled bags. There were food items in another bag, blankets and pacifiers in a third, medical supplies in a fourth, and extra clothing in a fifth. She did this for each of the children she sent to our house for respite. We were always quick to do overnight respites for her because we knew everything would be smartly packed together, labeled, and easy to find. We eventually adopted this method ourselves. Now, when our foster children come home from being away overnight, we open those gallon bags then inventory, clean, and restock them immediately for the next outing.

Another packing hint when leaving the house for the day is to pack a bed sheet and several strong binder clips. We construct makeshift items with the sheet, such as shades for naps, a pillow or blanket, a prop for a floppy-muscled child, or a diaper changing station. Another good idea is to change babies' bibs often during the day. This saves on the number of laundry loads we have to do because of outfit stains, and the children look fresh and clean longer. I avoid bibs with a Velcro closure because they pull and tangle children's hair at their neck, collect fuzz, and are easily pulled off by little hands. I buy only snap closure bibs.

One strategy that I find especially helpful the evening before a day outing is to announce the expected time everyone will need to be ready the next morning for "family loading time." This explicitly means that clothes have been approved as appropriate for the events of the day ahead of time, all shoes are located, teen hair is already done, and all the little ones are fed in preparation for loading. At the agreed-upon time, we expect that all family members are personally ready and on deck for cooperative loading, including last-minute leg braces applied, shoes tied, diaper blowouts changed, zippers zipped, car seats buckled, and strollers and wheelchairs loaded.

Conversely, when one adult is coming home from a day of running, the other family members already at home know they are an automatic member of the "welcome home committee." Everyone is expected to energetically greet the crew arriving home, share in the work of unpacking the bags, tidying the car, managing the high-energy transition time, restocking the supplies, and getting the children settled into the next activity. We cannot stress this strategy enough, especially when the person returning home has had a long day. Emphasizing a shared workload, along with plenty of praise for cheerful participants, makes this routine run smoothly, and maybe on some days it's a little fun too.

Lastly, we highly suggest not accepting more children into your care than you can drive around in your current vehicle. In the case of foster parents, sometimes that does not come to mind with the initial placement call. We took two young siblings in one night. Two weeks after placement, we were told that their mother was expecting again. Surprise, seven months later, we had both twin baby siblings placed with us too. Now, add in our own four biological children who were not of driving age yet, and we had to take two cars everywhere we went. Approved mileage to an event is for one vehicle only, so we had a big increase in gasoline bills for the next year until we finally gave in and bought a bigger vehicle.

ORGANIZATIONAL LISTS

Making detailed lists of what other caretakers need to know is a must. People have busy lives, including family and friends who might be helping us out with childcare. They appreciate directions being made clear and concise, which makes them more willing to help and leads to accurate care provided for often-complex children. Our lists inform about feeding issues, allergies, and of course copies of the no-thank-you requests.

To ensure accuracy and safety, we make lists regarding routines that need to be followed, such as medicine administration. We also make lists of everything that needs to be packed in a bag so that it can be repacked into the same bag with ease after an event. Making reusable organizational lists prevents items from being lost with the endless packing and unpacking of items that have been sent to school, daycare, respites, or visits. We would hate for a beloved blankie or a bottle of anti-seizure medicine to get left behind!

Parents know last-minute changes in plans offer little time to think through the details of caring for multiple children. Preparing ahead of time alleviates much of this problem. Six-month-old Ella had specific doctor-ordered feeding instructions. Due to her extreme obesity, specific amounts of formula were fed to her at set intervals. The list compiling these facts about her feeds was necessary, especially on the day the agency added another sibling group of three to be placed in our home with only an hour's notice. Ella needed to be taken to a foster friend's house for a few hours to give Ron and me time to regroup and get the new children settled. We would have been scrambling and most likely stressing trying to get all the bags packed and lists written had we not been prepared ahead of time.

For older children, we use lists to guide them and to demonstrate how to stay organized. Preteens Cheyenne and Miguel came from a home where their mother was severely drug dependent, and their lives were lacking any level of consistent routine from day to day. While the changes coming into foster care were extreme to the way they used to spend their days, they adapted readily and embraced the idea of having a list to follow. Miguel told me it made him feel important to have things to do. Cheyenne said having a list made her feel calm and safe because she knew what was happening that day. We had to have some written reminders for a while that started slowly with simple goals of a proper hygiene schedule for self-care and then moved on to higher-thinking activities that involved the use of calendars—like what days they would go to their aunt and uncle's house for a visit and what items they needed to take along with them. Packing to return to our house was easy too because they checked their lists to make sure all their items were remembered.

Lists can help keep order and help children's brains make sense of the details. Thankfully, Miguel was naturally goal-oriented and wanted out of the gruesome lifestyle he and his sister were forced into. He wanted to learn his school lessons, be on time with assignments, and know where he needed to be and when. He thought eventually that he might want a law enforcement career, which fit his rule-following personality. He said his goal was to be able to take care of his own family someday (including older sister Cheyenne).

Cheyenne was lucky that her brother was so dedicated to her, and even though she lacked that same level of motivation and organization, she did start to come out of her introverted shell and show interest in a tech career in animal care, which she took enough interest in to start researching online and making notes about. It was wonderful to hear her express feeling safe and come alive emotionally with the changes she was incorporating into her life. Her energy level, attitude, and momentum finally started heading upward.

CALENDARS

Formal family calendar meetings evolved from the need to increase our communication with each other. I use the term calendar loosely because our age-appropriate calendars range from pictures and scribbles to true adult organizational schedules. Calendars provide clear written communication and sequencing of events to help children adjust to the structured routine of a home. Specifically, we use calendar pages with pictures to help small children understand what is going around them, where they are going next, and which people they are involved with that day. We have been surprised at the excitement that surrounds these family calendar meetings and the banter and silliness the discussions bring.

We encourage all members of the family—regardless of age—to get involved in the calendar meetings. Younger children might sit with Foster Mommy or Foster Daddy and be their helper by scribbling on their own "calendar" coloring paper. School-aged children write in dates for school events, parental visits, practices, counseling, and church activities to personalize the calendar. Older children and young adults are shown how to use a calendar or day planner, in all their various forms, as a needed skill for the future. We compare our commitments a couple of times a month to add new events to the calendar and make sure each day will work logistically.

A preschooler we had placed with us several years ago thoroughly enjoyed going to the local Head Start Program in our town. He would jump up and down with excitement every day he saw the "goo bus" coming down the street to take him to class. His mother told me he previously had high absenteeism because in her area buses were not offered and she didn't have a dependable car to get him there every day. He was so thrilled to be able to consistently attend each day and watched his calendar like a hawk to make sure "Hoster Mommy" got him up for school on the right days. He took this responsibility seriously! With less truancy, he was an enthusiastic and natural learner.

One group of brothers literally had six people named "Jack" in their lives. Two counselors, a transportation aide, a case manager, their guardian ad litem, and a school friend (plus our dog!) were all named Jack. We had to give each Jack a nickname like Cheerful Jack, Driver Jack, and Friend Jack to keep the interactions straight. The children would identify each Jack by the way they chose to write in their calendars. The littlest brother used a happy face and a mad face to identify his two counselors.

We also started adding the children's visitation days with their families to the calendars. We used to think this was not a good idea because many times biological parents did not show up to the visits or the caseworker would call at the last minute to say the visit was canceled. We thought sparing the children's tears was easier by not keeping them fully informed and just surprising them with a visit if it really were to occur. Maybe this thinking was easier, on us at least, way back when. Now, with years of experience under our belts, we always add the visits in a different-colored pen, say orange. The children eventually learned that the events written in orange were appointments we hoped would happen but might not. This is a realistic lesson about the disappointments and losses that are a part of life. We are matter of fact about whatever happens and do not make a huge emotional deal about a missed visit, should it occur. I have not found lying to children about their parents' absenteeism to be helpful.

Early in our fostering career, one set of siblings placed with us multiple times was eventually put up for adoption. Along the way, many details of the mother's failed case plan were kept from the children, including why she rarely made visits. On the day the children were sat down together and told by their mother and the caseworker (I was behind the two-way glass) that they were not ever going home and were being adopted, they were in shock! The one little boy's emotional pleas of "What-what-what are you talking about?" still plays vividly in my mind. Decades later I still remember the shrill of the raw emotion in his cries like it was yesterday. He was incredulous with disbelief because he was not told the case plan had been failing at all. I learned a lesson that day about asking the caseworker to periodically explain, in an age-appropriate way, what is occurring with their case because in the end it is kinder not to blindside them with this life-changing news.

We also like to use calendars to help with countdowns because most children can process the timeline better if they can see what's happening on paper in front of them. If we go out of town and our children must stay with another caretaker, we give each child a paper with a calendar drawn out with the days we will be gone and when we will return. We ask the caregiver to help each child with their countdown. We always put a little gift sticker on the last day and bring a surprise of some sort back. After the last trip, we brought trick yo-yos for everyone.

In another case, we threw a going away party for one set of four siblings who had been placed with us for almost two years. The party was a big deal to them and of course the date of the party was put on all the children's calendars several weeks ahead of time. The cake read "Happy Graduation from Foster Care, Dante, Aisha, Clyde, and Marie!" They ran around the party showing the guests their special calendar pages and that both the party and reunification dates were listed. They were excited, proud, and loud the whole day! This event was a high point for our family not only because it was a fun closing day of a long successful case, but thanks to their special calendars, the children had a sense of order and routine knowing what was going on in their young lives.

NO-APPOINTMENT DAY

It is not unusual for us to have to squeeze five or six standing appointments into our weekly schedule with children. Examples of weekly appointments might include counseling, parental visits, therapies, speech class, and early intervention services. There are also doctor appointments. We have found it necessary to set aside a day each week and regard it as our day off. This "no-appointment day" approach helps us promote our longevity as parents and gives us a day to set aside for our own personal needs.

I typically do not schedule any appointments for Mondays. I have deemed this day my mental health day where I take time to clean up from our weekend activities, wrap my brain around the coming week's events, and catch up on my own work hours. In a society where we are constantly pushing our children and ourselves to succeed, we forget how important it is to have transition periods to allow our brains to relax, reset, and recover.

BUDDY SYSTEM

We like having meaningful outings and activities in our schedule. To not lose anyone while we are in a new place, we often will assign "buddies." Assigning an older buddy to a tot in the family teaches children to be kind and responsible. We teach our children to watch out for one another throughout the day. Of course, this is all done within reason of what a child sibling should do for another child sibling. Older siblings can learn organizational skills and be compassionate for younger children. Younger children can benefit by having a big brother or sister to look up to. One advantage of a blended family is the unique opportunity to be a big sibling one day and a little sibling the next, depending on which children are in the home on any given day.

Foster son Donte was the oldest sibling in his family of four. When he and his siblings moved in with us, he became a middle child when our biological children were added into the equation. He now had a big brother and three big sisters as well as his own three younger siblings. He enjoyed the newfound freedom and attention he got playing sports and occasionally doing "big kid" activities with older siblings. The mentoring relationship that developed with Matthew and Donte was very special to see too. For once, Matthew got to learn the role of an older child. The boys found common ground with their love of any sport. Matthew and Donte already had a lot of natural athletic talent, but having each other as buddies to play hours of ball helped their skills too.

Our biological children have also experienced the phenomenon of changing birth order in the family. One day, our eldest daughters Melissa and Katherine shifted from being the only children in our home to the position of younger siblings when older foster brothers Noah and Bruce joined our household. The girls loved having older brothers to play Ring Around the Rosie with and to bang on paint cans like drums as we renovated our house. These four still share a special bond decades later.

Oppositely, Matthew morphed to being the oldest in the whole house when his three older sisters went off to college and new, younger sibling groups would join the family. Matthew discovered newfound freedoms being the older sibling and was a good role model to the younger children in our home. I see it as an eye-opening advantage that everyone gets a temporary period of time to try a different position within the family. I feel like it gives us a nice appreciation for each other and helps us learn skills we wouldn't have had otherwise.

All positions in the buddy system teach understanding and tolerance of others, no matter which place in line the child falls. We, of course, have always given special attention to our dear biological children because being raised in a home alongside many foster children is such a unique upbringing and requires them to be adaptable to many day-to-day changes. Learning to adjust to change can be hard, but having to learn changing roles early in life also promotes maturity and resiliency. Some days they are all in with this vocation and other days they have their own needs to focus on. We remember that this degree of parenting is our undertaking not theirs.

When contemplating the buddy system in your home, be sure to incorporate children from another blended situation into *your* family, and be careful to not lose your family identity in the process. Try pairing children either formally or informally to help make the transition easier so the new child feels like they have a buddy. Have older children or even younger children who have been established longer at the home lead by example when welcoming newcomers.

We try to encourage buddies to keep us informed when they learn something specific like a special celebration or family traditions that come to their attention that we might be unaware of. Sharing new views or ideas from each of the children is the goal, but opening up to their buddy, instead of new parents, may be easier on the added child. We are happy to hear information about special family days, cultural traditions, or even concerns that their buddy can pass along to us. Having a well-matched buddy system in place helps ease the transition and acts as an added safety net.

Cheyenne and Miguel come immediately to mind when referring to the buddy system. They were so wounded emotionally when they came into foster care and were genuinely grateful for every life experience we provided for them. We shared the idea of the buddy system with them, being that our two college students were home for the holidays for several weeks and that Elizabeth and Matthew would help them get acclimated to our home routine as big buddies. Elizabeth and Matthew decided to take the children to the workout room at the YMCA their first week in care. Cheyenne accidentally spilled her water bottle while walking on the treadmill and told me when she got home that she couldn't believe Elizabeth didn't yell at her when she spilled her drink and instead cheerfully helped her clean it up. I was glad she had a buddy with her at the gym that day to ease the awkward incident.

SHOWER DETAIL

We instigated strict shower schedules into our routine long ago. Time separations provide an added degree of safety, modesty, and privacy—an important standard to instill in all children, especially ones older than age five. While we do not typically have unrelated teen girls and teens boys in our home together, this has occurred on several occasions. Also, unfortunately, we have had a couple of foster children who have sexually perpetrated on their own siblings, so since they are still typically placed into foster care together, they need a heightened level of monitoring too. In addition, there are our mama and papa bear hunches to be considered. In short, we are constantly counting to make sure all children are present and accounted for, especially when there are numerous older children from different families in the house.

What works well for us is having Ron monitor the older boys upstairs while the girls remain on the main floor in an activity of their choosing with me. Then the girls have their bathing times while I am upstairs doing laundry or other chores, and the boys watch TV in the family room with Foster Dad. We have a saying in our home that "modest is hottest," and this is one small rule that teaches children respect for the gift of the body that God has given to them. Several times, we had children from three separate families living in our home, and safety was constantly being managed with manipulating our environment, including having separate shower details.

As part of our shower-time routine, children are asked to set out clothes that are appropriate for the next day's planned events to ensure quick dressing time in the mornings. We get up at roughly the same time each day, go straight into morning hygiene time, and then start the day fully dressed and ready with beds made, which shows the first accomplishment of the day. We modify the wake-up time somewhat for teens, but this would not include sleeping in until noon or a four-hour afternoon nap. Daytime is for being awake and nighttime is for sleeping. If we have good preparation the night before, our mornings are less chaotic, and our days begin on a good note. I know families who chase their children around for hours each morning attempting to get every tooth brushed and onesie T-shirt changed. There is not enough time in my day for that style of parenting.

POTTY TRAINING

We even have a routine to potty train youngsters! Generally, for children of normal development, we begin potty training on the child's third birthday. At this age, children are ready to make the change to "big girl" or "big boy" underpants. We make a big deal of this highly anticipated day, which includes a trip to the store to pick out their favorite underpants. Children with nearly normal development have the understanding that these new special pants are not diapers. They also have the mind and bladder muscle maturity to be ready for this task. We do not go back and forth between underpants and diapers, so the children learn to take pride in keeping them clean. Once we switch to underpants, underpants it is! We do not revert to diapers at bedtime either; we use disposable Pull Ups with plastic pant covers over them and protective bed pads to prevent excessive linen changes while they are learning.

On the other hand, many children have developmental delays that result in a high incidence of potty issues long past their third birthday. While it is true that sometimes incontinence is just an immature bladder, this is not always the case, especially with children who have developmental delays. The best practice is to remember that some children are going to wet and soil their pants, beds, and maybe your carpet, no matter what their age if their delays are due to past traumas. They need time to work on battling their personal demons before bedwetting and soiling will subside.

We have been taught that adverse toileting habits happen because children have little control over the circumstances of their lives. However, where and when to go to the bathroom is one thing that they do have control over. Be aware that most children cannot tell adults any of this because they do not know why they are having accidents. So, realistically, how do we survive? We aim to understand the child's issues, dig deep for sustained patience, always carry extra supplies, use washable bed pads, and unemotionally carry on. I have to say that toileting accidents and clean ups are one of the circumstances that comes to my mind when kindhearted people say, "I could never be a foster parent. I could never give them up." I often think *If they only knew the inside scoop!*

If problems arise, I explain to the child's doctor which bathroom issues I am seeing and let them determine if there is any further need for medical attention. After that, I work on making the soiling a *non-issue*. I do not say these words lightly because if you are a parent living with this issue in your home you know how awful the day-to-day stress of this can be, but trust me, it is necessary to keep the emotions low. We teach the children how to properly dispose of their Pull Ups or wash their soiled linens (if old enough) and make no further remarks. I teach the other members of the household to do the same. I may go to my room later and grumble or roll my eyes, as my own stress relief, but never in front of the child because honestly for those few children who might have better control than they are demonstrating, if they sense it bothers the adults, they may continue the behavior on purpose.

During closing ceremonies at bedtime, especially if we have extra children staying in our home that night, we address children's general pottying instructions without singling out any one child. I remind them where the Pull Ups are located in the supply dresser and that sizes are clearly marked. They are all instructed to consider using bed pads on the beds as a precaution. They may or may not choose to take me up on this suggestion, but if they do have an accident there is far less insistence needed on my part to have them wash their linens and remake their beds because they knew about the choice they made the night before.

I choose to do this because we have had children as old as sixteen who wet at night, and this is not something they want to discuss. That's why making a few general announcements lets the child know that this is something we are well equipped to deal with and something they don't need to feel worried about. I have had foster parents pick up children from my house after a respite weekend, surprised when they hear from their child that they woke up dry. I think it has a lot to do with this low-drama handling of an embarrassing problem. These children often ask me if they can come back and stay with us again.

Sticker charts and promised rewards are often effective incentives for non-traumatized children, but some children are wetting and soiling for reasons other than lack of motivation. Children in foster care may have not only suffered from a lack of food, shelter, and supervision but may have only had a bucket to relieve themselves in. Additionally, they may have witnessed sexual abuse, violence, prostitution, rape, suicide, and murder (it's true). Wetting the bed in the grand scheme of things is not that big of a deal.

Parents must muster the compassion to know that the potty issues are most likely because of the immature stage of development that their mind is in, not their bladder. We had to educate ourselves on the insidious reasons behind some potty struggles before we learned to talk ourselves into being less bothered by it. Though it's very challenging, we finally evolved enough in our parenting skills and stopped attempting to control something we had no control over.

We had two boys, Mitchell and Ike, who really should have been over the bedwetting issues by the time they came to us at ages nine and twelve. However, they were victims of sexual abuse in their younger years, which was likely the cause behind the bed wetting. Finally, after two years in care, both were having more dry nights than wet. On dry mornings, we met their elated faces with the comment, "Way to go!" They do not get a trophy for meeting the goal of staying dry, but we keep the praise targeting the feeling of satisfaction of their own success.

We try to remember the confusion the children are experiencing and do not add to their trauma by berating them. When the child is ready, bathroom control habits will eventually correct themselves. Being foster parents, we may never see the child meet this goal in the time they are with us, so instead we center our attention on knowing that there will be *some* days of dry beds, and for that we are thankful. We try to live up to the words of little three-year-old Mae Mae who always clapped her hands and chanted, "happy home, happy home" every time we pulled in the driveway. A happy home is achieved by not fighting unnecessary battles and instead giving children a good childhood experience.

CHAPTER 10: PLAYFULNESS

We were in no way prepared for the fact that we would have to teach children *how* to play when we became foster parents. This sounds ridiculous, but it is true. Destructive "play" is the norm for many children. They throw games, rip books, break action figures apart, use any toy as a weapon, and constantly scream monster sounds and killing phrases. In full force, the level of violence is shocking to see. They have very little experience with side-by-side cooperation with peers, and they role play and pretend in inappropriate ways.

THE ART OF PLAY

Every week, foster son Jayden, age five, would purposefully rip the soles off his tennis shoes as we traveled the thirty minutes from our home to the visit center to see his mom. He thought he was "playing" and keeping himself entertained by ripping his shoes apart when, really, he was being destructive. He exhibited anxiety, stress, and anger, plus he hated being confined to a car seat since he had not been in one routinely while in his mother's care. I finally figured this out after two weeks straight of leaving home with intact shoes and arriving thirty minutes later with soleless tennis shoes. From then on, he traveled in the car seat in socks, holding an indestructible squishy ball instead, and we put his shoes on when we arrived at the destination.

The rudimentary skill of play must be demonstrated. Limits are set until good play habits are formed. We instruct with phrases such as: "We do not play killing each other with guns or scare like monsters in this house because toys are not meant to be used this way." We interrupt this type of play every time it happens until the proper use of play develops. We demonstrate this by sitting on the floor with the child and teaching them less violent ways to play. We will spend quiet time with them too and not quiz or question their thought process but just be present with them. Some children need years of follow-through to understand the art of reasonable play because they were not exposed to supervision early on.

We did a one-week respite for a family who discouraged television watching in their home. The children generally watched about an hour's worth of children's programming only once a day. While this minimal TV time was a little bit extreme for us, we did notice that these little girls were incredibly kind to each other and were creative in their imaginary play. They were well spoken and smart. When we turned the TV on ourselves, they would politely move themselves to another room to play! Their favorite activity was taking small toy figures and building a story around the pieces on the table. We were tremendously impressed with their level of quality playtime and learned firsthand about incorporating less screen time and more interactive play in our routine.

In addition, we make a big effort to keep children moving during their play hours. Forts, treehouses, ninja obstacle courses, splash pools, and scooters make for great outdoor fun. Tumbling mats, mini ball courts, balance boards, and walking stilts are fun indoor options. Ron frequently organizes games of basketball, baseball, or football while teaching the fair rules of the games. For our friends fortunate enough to have acreage for children to run around and play on, we appreciate the times they share their resources with us. Promoting physical movement and imagination play keeps children busy, prepares them for cooperation as they grow, provides a fun outlet for their energy, and keeps their minds growing.

As we choose to limit the time that children use electronics, we also make sure that electronics and video games are not the only fun activity they have available to them. We do offer time after homework, dinner, and chores for the children to use the electronic entertainment. We have found that once the children are over the shock of not having endless screen time, they enjoy active playtime, especially outdoors, as well as reading before bed to promote better sleep.

We rotate our toys based on children's developmental needs. When children are overwhelmed by too many toys in front of them, they cannot decide what to play with and instead scatter the toys everywhere. When their toys are broken and disorganized, their play typically follows the same mindset. We sort small toys into gallon bags and put them up in a cupboard to combat thousands of mismatched pieces of toys all around our house. All the pieces are together, safe from the mouths of the little ones, and the toys feel new when a child asks to play with them. In turn, our children know to clean up one toy bag before they get another down. We have found this to be extremely helpful in cutting down on cleaning time with toys and keeping our toys nice for years. We can realistically allow for toy cleanup to be placed on their no-thank-you list because the small toys we keep out are minimal.

We also teach that toys are only for play and not for eating. I know, again this seems obvious. Children will eat crayons, chalk, Play-Doh, and sand. They do not chew these items for oral exploration but are rather literally eating these items because some had no other options at home when they were hungry. One little girl we had ate pebbles and chalk frequently. We had to keep a very close eye on her when we were outside playing. Still, her diapers revealed that she did consume chalk and pebbles on occasion.

One set of siblings used to leave their home daily while their mother was sleeping. They would walk the four blocks alone down the street to a park to play. Lyndsey (four) and Jacob (two) crossed two busy roads on their way to the park. I was told by the social worker that there were only dirty broken toys in the rundown yard at the place they stayed, which did not keep them occupied while their mother was frequently passed out from various binges. The children's only real opportunity for play was the park down the road. They were brought into the foster-care system when a neighbor continued to call children's services to complain about the children eating cat food off her porch and crossing busy roads alone. She was rightly concerned about the potential dangers of this lack of supervision.

PINT-SIZED TOYS ON THE GO

The art of distracting children is made easy by carrying small, prepackaged toy bags in a purse or bag. We make pint-sized zipper bags ahead of time with small fun toys that are easy to grab and go when we are on the run. One bag has a little dog veterinarian set. Another has miniature baby dolls with bottles. We have superhero figures and miniature sets of books. Building sets, ink stampers, and stencil kits are a favorite, so we have several of those. These special toy baggies are kept only for trips out of the house. They are fresh activities that offer a great distraction when needed, and none of them need a charger!

Some parents are losing out on the opportunity to talk to their children, and children are learning they have to be entertained nonstop with the use of electronic devices. Toy bags are a great conversation starter at a restaurant or while waiting for an appointment time rather than losing a child to a screen. So often, I notice teenaged children with an earbud in their ear while out to dinner with their family. While they only have one in their ear so they "can still hear you," they are clearly distracted by their own entertainment. Having real dinner conversation helps children and families communicate effectively.

One day we were waiting our turn to be called in for our appointment at the pediatrician's office. I got out several of our toy bags with cars, action figures, and tiny baby dolls and puppies to play alongside of my several small children. Before long, every child in the waiting room was seated at my feet participating. Children are not as interested in watching reruns on Mom's phone as we tend to think and instead thoroughly enjoy the interactive playtime with an adult.

Another time while heading into the optometrist's office for our children's routine eye exams, the secretary stopped me and told me she had one of the small books from our princess book set that had been left there the year before. She had remembered my family and the bagged toys from previous years' visits with other children, and she knew the book had to be ours. It took a whole year, but we eventually got our favorite set of miniature books back together!

A huge decline has been seen in youngsters regarding verbal and social skills over the past decade. Speech therapists tell me that the lack of parents having day-to-day conversation with their children is the reason why. Coaching children and their families about this decline and what they can do about it is a big part of our mission so that they, in turn, can pass good parenting skills on to future generations.

Children have lots of extra energy, especially at the exact moment they are being asked to be quiet and sit still, like in a doctor's office or at a restaurant. Preparing the children ahead of time and grabbing premade toy bags provides an easy and inexpensive way to pass the time and promote play and language skills too.

THE COOPERATION STATION

We have come up with a few helpful hints for parenting multiple children of similar ages who have a hard time playing nicely together. Some children are constantly antagonizing each other, and every small infraction is met with a bloodcurdling scream. To curb this behavior, we use "station time" where we separate the children into different play spaces or stations until they become better at cooperative peer play. While one child plays on the floor with the racetrack, one is in the tall-top chair with Play-Doh, and another is on the mini jungle-gym set in the playroom. We set up different activities and then rotate turns through.

Next, we let them try to play together on their own for short periods of time. If the poor behavior returns, station time begins again. Sometimes, the separation and gathering attempts go on for days. Once some small form of cooperative interactive play is achieved, we catch their good behavior, praise them, and reduce the restrictions. The need for adults to prompt tolerable play will decrease as the children get used to managing play on their own.

Because traumatized children usually come from chaotic homes, learning cooperative play and dispute resolution is difficult. Four-year-old Devon hauling off and punching two-year-old Justin in the face almost every time the younger brother got within three feet of his toy was not appropriate play. Even though I am a fan of letting children settle some disputes independently, this was not going to work in our house. We are forever telling children of all ages that if they can learn to play cooperatively with their siblings and peers, then naturally other people will enjoy being around them more too.

Cooperation also comes into play for children in other environments. For foster children, visiting with their parents at the visit center tends to be loud, crowded, and overstimulating. We teach the children cooperative play skills in the foster home in the hopes that they will carry these new skills with them and play well when they are with their parents. Teaching the children cooperative play, how to settle small disputes independently, and how to comfort each other's small hurt feelings without turning into a full-fledged blowup can lead to a better visit. Better visits can lead to successful case plan goals being met. Completion of case plans is what gets children home and reunited with their families again. For children who can understand, we explain that this is one small way they can help get themselves home.

I recently watched a news report that delved into why a child is seen as popular by their peers. The children who were asked denied good grades, athletic prowess, and socioeconomic status as important and instead more often than not characterized popular kids' dispositions as "nice" or "cooperative." These "popular" teens themselves, when interviewed, said that they liked all their classmates and did not remember going to school with any children they disliked. This makes sense; that is why we bring to our children's attention the importance of being kind to each person they meet.

Acceptable peer behavior is a needed skill whether the child is a tot or a teen. As adults, we can help significantly by being consistent in our expectations for cooperation. The same rules for fair play in childhood are the same rules for excelling as adults in the real world. Youngsters who can play cooperatively together when young will be a friend to a peer as a teen and progress on to being a cooperative member of society as an adult.

SENSORY PLAY

Sensory play helps a child's brain grow by using their five senses. At an appointment years ago, a neurologist explained to me what is commonly called sensory processing deficit. With this condition, information goes into the child's brain, but it is not seen, heard, smelled, felt, or tasted as it is in a child with no sensory delays. Children with a trauma can have an even higher degree of difficulty decoding the information the brain is trying to absorb and understand. Common ways that trauma manifests itself in children is through sensory delays such as covering their ears when they hear a routine loud sound, disliking a scratchy tag on their clothes, or being a picky eater, to name a few. It is common for children with sensory issues to be overstimulated and therefore frequently have dramatic reactions. They have meltdowns even with the simplest requests.

Effective parents help counterbalance delays by involving children in new types of play activities that stimulate their five senses. Since part of our favorite activities is out-loud reading time, we find different ways to expose the children to this reading fun. One day we had the children take their books up in the tree house for reading time and another day Kaye floated around on the raft with her novel. Reading a book to a child yourself is a different experience for the child's brain than having them read independently with a flashlight under a blanket at nighttime. A child coloring a picture sitting in a chair at the table is a different experience for the brain than the child sitting under the table coloring a picture that is taped to the top of the table. Taking a dance class or learning an instrument can strengthen an area of the brain that might be lagging behind. Each of these examples help form new connections in the brain with every new experience the child has.

My own four children decided one day they wanted to color under the table. I gave them permission for this, as it would be a new activity that seemed harmless. To my surprise, they didn't use the paper and tape provided and colored on the actual table! I now had a beautiful artwork mural drawn on the table's underside. And since the damage was done, the children often colored under the table, adding to their masterpiece. To this day, I still have the table because I can't bring myself to part with this wonderful memory.

Stimulating a child's sense of hearing is also easy and fun. Toys are found throughout our house that stimulate creative music play. Hands down, a favorite activity for two of our little ones, Skye and Caleb, was their music therapy sessions at the hospital. For example, Skye, who was nonverbal due to her handicaps, would not only listen to the therapist play a sound on the guitar and watch the lady's facial expressions change as her mouth formed words but would also feel the vibrations on the wood of the body of the guitar with her hands. Her excitement and joy were infectious to witness. These toddlers transformed from lackluster patients lying in hospital beds surrounded by beeping medical equipment into lively, silly personalities that swayed, smiled, bounced, and cooed with joyful noises with the strumming of the instrument. This was a nice break in their day and gave the children something else to focus on rather than being ill.

The therapist commented that she felt Skye was more taken by her music therapy than any other child she had ever helped. I would love to see music therapy become more widely used, but for now I adapt and use what I learned from their therapy classes into fun rhythm bands in our home. Also, we have found a significant decrease in children bickering with each other when background classical music is played in our playroom. Music is a source of stress relief, a great coping skill, AND it helps keep the chaos noise down.

Feeling the sensation of water is a form of play that children cannot resist. Bathtubs, sprinklers, pools, and playing "dishes" at the kitchen sink are our go-to activities on a daily basis, and they bring excitement to the children. Caleb had many handicaps, delays, and was nonverbal. Besides cuddling and snuggling, nothing pleased him more than playing in a sink full of water. In fact, I would prepare supper on the counter next to him while he sat in the kitchen sink letting the water run over his hands and arms and repeatedly filling different-sized containers with water. Recently, I saw a mom who put a large basin of warm water under her toddler's bare feet as the child was playing in a jumpy seat suspended from a doorway. What a great idea for water fun! I am storing that ingenious idea away for the next baby I care for!

Vary the ideas and activities and adjust them to your child's specific needs, skills, or handicaps. My foster friend Francis is always singing, dancing, and talking up a storm with her little ones. She is constantly doing activities to expand the children's experiences. She actively cooks and gardens with youngsters and lets her older children ride their bikes and scooters rain or shine. They paint with rags, sponges, and marbles. There is a loud and loving mess over at her place, but she does have intelligent and creative children.

We ask older children what things they like to "play" with to feel happy and we try to provide these activities for them. The older children are always asking Ron to play basketball or baseball with them outside. They also love having their own craft boxes filled with paints and textiles. The adult-sized punching bag in the basement is a favorite. Each child is encouraged to pursue whichever activities are most interesting to them.

Some people consider sensory play the "Montessori Way" where children's play is considered their work. I am a big fan of weaving all sorts of sensory-stimulating ideas into my individualized parenting plan for each child, where hands-on learning, natural abilities, and interests are encouraged. Helping the child develop real-world experience through as many clever parenting ideas as possible is the goal.

DAD TIME

Dad's attention is the best! Many children do not have active fathers in their daily lives. Sadly, we know some children who do not know their fathers even after many DNA tests have been submitted. Having absent dads is crippling our society. An active father or father figure in a child's life will significantly curb many of the child's problems. A father's affection and support has been shown to positively affect a child's cognitive and social development. Early patterns that develop because of time spent with a father figure help children develop a sense of what is acceptable and loving in a relationship. The lessons learned by positive male interactions will project forward to other relationships the child has later in life.[7]

A crucial piece of a child's foundation is having a father figure to talk with, learn from, and be responsible to. Children need male role models to show them how to give a firm handshake, hold the door open for a lady or someone with their hands full, give up a seat for an elder, and learn young lady and gentlemanly respect. Several of the middle school and high school boys we keep in contact with will have a "bring your dad to practice night" or "Doughnuts with Dad Day" at school. Ron has attended many of these days throughout the years. One of our younger foster sons once sadly told us, "I don't have a dad to go with." Ron reminded him that he has a foster dad now. Not infrequently, he gets asked to attend these special events even after the children leave our care because of this strong emotional connection he has with them. There are many girls and boys who have passed through our home who still consider him a father figure in their life, long after they have left our home.

One summer day, the ice cream truck came down the street in our neighborhood and the many cries for purchases started. Ron spoke up, "Let's go outside and get a game of running bases going instead." Soon after, I got ice cream cups out of the freezer. Not only had physical activity been started and already-bought snacks consumed, but the ice cream truck's melody faded away without protests. While giving in to the ice cream snack would have been easier and something we do treat the children to on occasion, getting a ball game started gave Ron better bonding time with the children.

I often say we are happily collecting a lot of children. We love watching them play and create experiences in foster care. It is spectacular to watch their play develop in our home with the tips and tricks we teach them. Just as the chapters in each child's life changes, our support for them from rudimentary play to cooperative interactions with their peers never wavers.

CHAPTER 11: AS THEY GROW

Children need the support of parents far beyond the age of eighteen. As children grow, their parental needs will change. While we were once changing diapers and making sure our little ones had food to eat, now we might be offering a listening ear about a hard day at work or financial advice. In one way or another, we will continue to support our children our whole lives.

INCLUSION

We are big supporters of inclusion with every child we encounter. Exclusion is an incredibly strong emotion and is a feeling we have all experienced. Finding a clever, unassuming way to include a child is a sentiment that adds a layer of love and acceptance no matter how small the gesture. Something even as silly as, "Hey, Katie! You're wearing a blue shirt today too, just like Foster Dad and me! We can all be members of the blue shirt club today." Just a small gesture like this gives a child a momentary boost.

One simple practice we learned from camp sleepovers in scouts is to have the children arrange their sleeping bags with their heads in a circle and their feet spanned outward to make the shape of a flower. This is an ingenious way to prevent excluding a child from the sleeping arrangement. With the flower petal design, all children present are friends and there is no need for groups or cliques. Adjusting the details, this idea is an effective way to decrease the chances of anyone being left out and helps keep children's defenses down and emotions even.

One hot day while our family was at the park, we spotted a few of our preteen foster daughter's classmates hanging out there as well. They had not reached out to twelve-year-old Leslie to invite her to play with them, and she was too hesitant to approach the trio. As we sat our oversized family of ten down in a circle, we shouted over a welcome greeting to the girls, while waving colorful popsicles overhead, and asked them if they would like to join us. Thankfully, they happily ran over and joined us for the cool treat. Leslie was thrilled, and as we dispersed, they asked her to hang out with them at the swings for a while. This day served as proof that adults need to encourage opportunities from which children benefit.

Diversity is a wonderful idea when it is approached fairly and organically. We have experienced nothing but positivity having children from over a dozen countries pass through our home. We view cross-cultural and cross-racial fostering as a blessing. It has provided us with unique friendships and chances to learn. This does not mean that there are not cultural differences to get used to, because there certainly are. We listen to foster children and their families as they talk about things that are important to them, about food they eat or avoid, which days they celebrate as holidays, and we share our thoughts with them. Culture exists inside cultures as well. They exist between families, lifestyles, and neighborhoods. We show great respect to all in our home because this is what we want to do, not because someone is telling us to. We do our best to follow through when we ask the child how we can help make them feel comfortable and safe. Inclusion is all powerful irrespective of nationality, culture, or beliefs.

Embracing coparenting with the "other set of parents" (fosters/divorced/blended) and including them as much as possible decreases the stress on the children because they do not have to choose sides. Inclusivity might be hard on the adults, but how the children feel is most important. So even if the other parents do not reciprocate, we embrace their family as much as possible. A safe and accepting home deepens children's roots, strengthens their emotional foundation, calms negative behaviors, and gives them positive experiences as they grow.

HILLS AND VALLEYS

Insisting on a home environment where extreme emotional ups and downs are frowned upon takes determination and willpower, especially with preteens and teens. Outbursts usually start with an escalation, and emotions spiral out of control. The child then goes into survival mode which manifests itself in pouting, hitting, screaming, withdrawing, or even self-harm. We do our best to tame this world of emotional chaos with our parenting skills.

I would say that the extreme ups and downs of children's emotions is one of the biggest reality checks of being a parent because the duration and frequency can be exhausting. Honestly, part of embracing the life of a parent is understanding that at the end of a stressful work week parenting does not stop. There is no concrete finish line in seeing behaviors improve either. We move along with one emotional foot in front of the other hoping to have the stamina and experience to deal with the aftermath of each problem as it occurs.

Having giant reactions to small incidents is common with children who are stressed. But there are many opportunities to creatively minimize stress. LaToya would routinely throw herself on the floor screaming and crying "no, no, no" when an outfit she did not want to wear was suggested. The level of drama did not fit the situation. To rise above the noise and confusion, she picked out clothes at the same time each evening and we learned to manipulate the environment by having specific clothes in the dirty laundry basket when we did not want a particular item worn. Two or three acceptable outfit choices were given each evening for her to pick from, along with setting the rule that clothing changes cannot be made in the morning. In hindsight, she might have a future as a thespian because once we set these limits the drama immediately stopped. Looking back, it seemed a lot like a show.

One way to help children compartmentalize stressful situations is to downplay the "poor me" factor. Demonstrating how to power through stress and find support is what well-adjusted families do. We model that we do not let the lows get us down for an excessively long period of time. Now, I am not referring to diagnosed depression but day-to-day happenings in most people's lives. We all have stress as a part of our history, but after a time of processing, mourning the loss or disappointment, and healing, these stresses do not get to define us in the long term. Who we choose to become, with the intertwining of all our life experiences, makes each of us uniquely who we are today.

Only child Lee had a difficult childhood growing up with her mother's daily drug and alcohol use. She also had the tragic loss of her dear grandparents from an accident when she was ten. She was a profoundly sad girl. Lee's counselor concentrated her therapy on how to compartmentalize her sadness, mourn her losses, take up a hobby, and over time also allow herself to be happy again. Along with being followed by a psychiatrist, Lee worked on processing her unspoken thoughts and feelings and imagined being victorious over her problems instead of endlessly focusing on the victim role. Happiness is a choice. She had to eventually choose to be happy again. After a hard year in therapy, she joined the high school drama club, made new friends, started having fewer ups and downs, and her emotional strength was more even keel.

Children are not going to say, "I'm really struggling with some tough emotions now, and I'm not sure how to cope." They are going to act out in challenging ways, but it means the same thing. A nonthreatening comment of support might sound like, "It looks like things aren't going well for you right now. Want to tell me what you're thinking?" The best advice I have is to listen to the child, piece together bits of information, pay attention to their body language, and offer to help the child find coping skills that they themselves feel will help them. I do not automatically try to solve their problems for them.

We notice what each child uses as their go-to coping skill and guide them to consider other options if their choices are unhealthy. Buck used the punching bag in the basement when he was frustrated. Davy needed to be outdoors where he could climb trees, ride his skateboard, and be loud through physical activity. Autumn liked to research certain places or people and draw about them in her journal. Beth preferred quiet, thoughtful time to focus on music and prayer. Empowering children with coping strategies to decrease escalations also gives them a degree of satisfaction that they know what to do to help themselves feel better and have a practiced skill to fall back on when life gets tough.

Coaching children on how to handle difficult situations before they occur helps to avoid the hills and valleys of extreme responses. When we are headed to the hospital for an evaluation from the doctor, I will explain to the child everything that is happening and will assure them that I will listen to them and will stay near them. I also do not lie to the child. I may say, "It is likely that the nurses will be drawing a blood sample from your arm. It's okay to cry but not to scream. These people are trying to help you." I keep in mind that when children are exposed to trauma it influences how their brains are wired and how they react to an appointment like this, so I provide extra tender loving care.

When it comes to the hills and valleys of emotions, I have learned to expect the unexpected. I once had a six-year-old foster daughter who had been well prepared for the routine pediatrician evaluation appointment ahead of time, but once we got to the child-friendly facility she fell to the ground, started screaming, and held onto a table leg in the waiting room for dear life. I assured the staff that she did not need them to overreact by hovering over her, bribing and pleading with her to come in. I asked them to leave the area, and I would sit with Johanna on the floor until she was over this outburst. With a quiet voice that was in control, I explained to Johanna again why we were there that day and let her have a few minutes to regain her composure without the audience of well-meaning staff. Once she felt we could restart, we went on with the appointment. For whatever reason, her brain decided to go the route of extreme emotional overload even though I had done all I could think to do to prepare her for the appointment.

To help the children stay in reasonable control of their emotions, my goal is to anticipate their trauma triggers, avoid them if possible, and learn strategies to reduce their effect if they happen anyway. Once a child has more experience dealing with their triggers, the coping strategies will become an integrated and useful part of the child's life. They might use the strategy when in distress or just as a reset to get back on track with their day.

The schoolteacher meant well when offering Wayne a stuffed animal bribe to get on the school bus one day as he was having a meltdown with this routine request. The bribe worked for one day. The problem was that he then wanted a prize every day for getting on the bus—an expected task that all the third graders were asked to do. He told the bus driver that he needed to have a toy. That seemed a bit extreme since he had been riding the bus without problems the previous months before. We had the tough love "life goes on" talk about doing what he needs to do to get to and from school because the alternative was missing school and doing the homeschool option of classes at home all day, with no peer classmates, no fun playground, and with Foster Mom being the teacher. He got over his bus riding issues quickly. I informed the bus driver about his options and choices, and she started expecting much better behavior from him, which he provided. This was also a great opportunity to explain to Wayne that the other students on the bus probably did not enjoy his antics and that his behavior delayed them from getting home on time. We talked about being a better friend, and this was a good way to start.

DE-ESCALATION

Helping a child de-escalate or calm down after an event of high emotion is an important step to helping children grow emotionally. Emotional meltdowns happen. Restorative conversations help the child regain control, process what happened, and regulate their feelings back to normal. Sometimes children can explain why they reacted the way they did after everything calms down.

In Johanna's case with the table-clutching incident in the office waiting room, I found out that this was the same hospital where she had had a liver biopsy test done the year before (not a pleasant test). I had no idea about this at the time. In my opinion, this was a good reason for the meltdown. Focusing on the bounce back, I did empathize with her story (once I was able to figure out what she was talking about) and acknowledged how difficult that day must have been for her. I also restated the expectations about how to let me know if she is scared in a way that I can better understand the next time.

We explain to children that in the real world not every detail of a stress can be explained to them before it happens. There are stresses that are out of everyone's control. This is the reason helping them know that very high highs and very low lows do not help them cope well in the long run. To get through an unexpected stress, it is better to try to gather as much information from what is going on around them, stay calm, ask for help if they need it. Our fallback is when all else fails, have grit, and just try your best.

OWE A NO

The idea to "owe a no" came from the need to train our adult brains to have a quick go-to response when emotions are at an unwanted high, we are nearing losing control, or there is a need for an immediate stop. This response works to quickly de-escalate a situation and will help a child or teen learn to back down once this discipline is taught and followed through a time or two.

When a situation is fraught with emotion, such as a teen wanting to throw valuable objects across the room, I state quickly, "If you choose to throw that, I will owe you a no." I wait and see which action they choose. Hopefully, they choose to stop the negative behavior. If they do not, I will immediately owe a no in response to the child's action, such as loss of a promised fun day at the water park with peers. The punishment will always match the crime. Big issues have big consequences, whereas small issues have smaller consequences. I redeem the removal of privilege in a timely manner, usually within a day or two. The first time the technique is used will likely not register for the child and will result in a loss of privilege for them, so I suggest using it in a small matter to teach the concept first. I follow through no matter what, which makes the technique very effective.

Candace was large in stature and physically aggressive. She threw items and swore when she was mad, followed by stomping around the house for hours to make sure everyone remembered how cross she was. When we were feeling frustrated, Ron or I would tell her, "Either get your feelings calmed down and stop pounding around the house or I owe you a no tomorrow when it is time for you to go to the movies." She would usually be persuaded to calm down because, like any teen, she wanted to spend time with her friends at the movies and she knew we would keep our word.

Owing a no can also be effective if a child does not want to start a task they have been given. I decide on a time frame that I am willing to wait and then I use the phrase. For example, "I have from 3 till 4 pm today to help you sort your summer clothes. After that I will clean your room myself and owe you a no." If I must do the chore, the next time the child asks for a privilege I remind them that I owed them a "no" from the previous day when they chose to have me sort clothes in their room instead of doing the task themselves. I think the owe a no discipline is effective because it quickly de-escalates drama and avoids a power struggle. The child is making the choice.

Again, our school-aged foster daughter Maya enjoyed baking; however, her downfall was that she routinely left the bathroom a complete mess. The owe a no technique was effective with her because she did not like losing her baking privileges. I would comment, "Feel free to start your cupcakes as soon as the bathroom has been tidied." I had to follow through with removing baking privileges a couple of times, but eventually she caught onto the idea. I paired this approach with a comment about how she was part of our family and tidying the bathroom after herself was a task that was expected of all family members in our home. She eventually developed a sense of belonging with our family and the messes became less of an issue. After being reunited with her father eighteen months later, she returned for four consecutive years to visit us and bake a birthday cake in preparation for her special day. She told me that she used this same technique at home with some of her eight younger brothers and sisters.

COMMUNICATION SKILLS

Technology is a blessing and a curse. We have a great many conveniences because of technology, yet verbal and social skills are suffering immensely, especially in children and teens, in part because of it. We have parented many children who do not understand the basic verbal skills they need to use to communicate. Learning communication skills, beyond texting, is imperative. Verbal conversation improves the child's maturation of speech, language, vocabulary, and thinking. The etiquette of good communication is critically important.

Being an active and polite listener should be brought to children's attention. Everyone knows someone who finishes the sentences of the person they are talking to. Our foster son Sam's dad was this way. He was so antsy to comment on the case manager's comments that half the time he missed what was being said. He also had a habit of one-upping every comment made to him. Instructions were repeated over to him, and directions were written down in case he was more of a visual learner, but even that did not help because he was already on to his next thought. It was exhausting answering his texts for details on the case after visits because all of this had been exchanged just a few minutes earlier. Clearly, lack of communication is an adult thing as well.

We explain that actively listening means not only what is being said but squelching the desire to make a follow-up comment prematurely before the first person is done talking. Only after listening and briefly commenting on the first statement of the conversation can the next verbal response be politely added. We do practice this with some children who need a little extra understanding of this concept.

Our energetic and chatty twelve-year-old Bianca benefited from a few communication prompts. She did not know about being an active listener, but she certainly had no trouble talking. We had her practice waiting until the speaker finished their comment and only then could she make an appropriate response back. This took some time to develop. She had to learn to pause and think a moment before she blurted out a response, which as a child diagnosed with attention-deficit/hyperactivity disorder (ADHD) was a skill she really had to work on. When she reunified with her biological family, we received a handwritten thank-you note from her stepdad, where he commented that this listening and responding skill alone had made a big difference in their ability to communicate with each other.

We are seeing so many speech delays due to a lack of verbal conversation. Parents spend too many hours in front of their devices, not looking at or talking with their children and teens. I believe mask wearing has also influenced small children's language learning because they cannot clearly hear what is being said. They cannot watch how the speaker forms the words through lip reading and have lost the facial expressions obstructed by a mask. Talking to and singing with children are two ways to combat these losses.

Chanting nursery rhymes, poems, and songs about opposites, colors, numbers, and letters helps with interpersonal interactions and speech and language development. When eight-month-old Mace would touch his nose, the speech therapist would look him in the eye about twelve inches from his face and say, "Mace is touching his nose. I'm going to touch my nose too." When he clapped his hands together, she replied, "Mace and Miss Sue are clapping hands together!" She said babies learn language and communication through kind repetition of what they are doing and verbal descriptions of their actions.

We train children in nonverbal communication as well. Posturing, gestures, facial expressions, and eye contact should also be pointed out as polite and effective communication skills. We bring body language to a child's attention if needed.

Seven-year-old Braelyn had an opinionated stance that screamed "get away from me," and she had perfected it. It included folded arms, a scowl on her face, and eyes staring down or rolling back. She modeled this pose at almost any request, even simple ones. We explained how an open stance with arms down and eyes up along with a pleasant look on her face would make her seem more approachable to others. Her counselor at weekly appointments emphasized the same skills. When she would complain about not having friends, she was reminded of her body language habit and was encouraged to smile more instead.

Communication also develops from reading to children. Reading helps speech and language develop and increases vocabulary. Further, reading enhances comprehension through better thought processing. Children as well as parents need to keep learning every day. Many parents know that a vast majority of a child's brain growth happens by the time they are three years old and that reading stimulates this brain growth, but most do not know that it is equally as important in keeping our brains from shrinking as we age.[8]

We have had teens who silently drift into the nursery in the evening when we are having nightly reading time with our younger children, just to sit and listen. They are welcomed with a smile and head nod, so they feel included but not embarrassed with too much attention being drawn to them. Sometimes teens are not fluid readers, so being read to can help with reading proficiency and bonding all at the same time. We cannot overstate the importance of reading daily at every age.

Encouraging children in the proper use of verbal communication skills will help empower them to become better prepared for the social demands of the adult work world. I asked my scouts to call and speak to me personally with RSVPs to campouts or other events to give them some practice with this skill. It was challenging for a few of them, but occasionally I will run into one of these girls, now adults, and they will bring up my insistence on responding verbally and say that they felt it helped them in preparing for the work world they are in today. I am often heard saying to teens that a smile, polite attitude, and strong communication skills are the important qualities that employers are looking for.

The best type of communication—and my personal favorite—might just be "front porch sittin'"! I think this is a bit of a lost art. Spending time together under the guise of more family interaction and less media gives a needed boost to preserving our families from all the media influence affecting most of us. Swinging on the porch, going to church together, daily phone calls, and family mealtime are outstanding activities for families to strive toward, and they build stronger family ties and better interpersonal connections.

Staying connected with each of your children is of paramount importance. Know what kind of communication each of your children prefers, then call, text, or visit them daily. It's a commitment and hard work, but they appreciate the kindness, as they understand that we are thinking about them and that the events of their life are meaningful to us. It's the best way to stay in tune with how they are doing. No matter their age, children need their parents or a parent-like figure in their lives to check in on them and provide accountability.

MEDIA USAGE

Cell phones have not been kind to parenting skills and are a hot topic between parents and children. Teens and young adults who solely use text messaging and social media for communication unintentionally stunt the growth of their communication, language, and social skills. Non-traumatized children may do okay on their own regarding self-limits, but traumatized children can lack that self-regulation factor and need more parental guidance.

Some of our basic suggestions regarding preteen and teen cell phone usage is to have them "based" in the kitchen, which means they are still accessible to the teens but are not in their pockets all day either. We think many problems are headed off if there is a nondramatic routine drop of the devices when they come home. Homework time is pretty much off limits for cell phone usage. If they need to look something up briefly, that's okay, but it should not be a constant thing. We have no phones at dinnertime and have the children follow others' rules about cell phone usage when at school or are over at a friend's house. We try to state these types of requests in a positive way such as, "We want to see your smiling face and interact with you when you are home. We miss you during the day!" They don't love it, but that's okay, that is the job of an active parent.

In our case, foster children's families decide if they can have a cell phone (and provide it) or not but we, the foster parents, make the parameters for its use in our home. We find that having no technology before school hours works best for us because most teens are getting out of bed at the last minute, so they do not have time to text excessively before school. We do allow limited cell phone time, which goes something like "Your cell phone time is from 4-8 pm, so after you do your homework, you may call your mom or play games or both, if you choose." I find for myself that I can tolerate monitoring during these hours the best. Eliminating phones in the bedrooms and keeping them in family community spaces is one routine we start as soon as children come into our home.

One of our teens came home from high school in a frenzy and threw her phone on the kitchen table. Ron, trying to be sly and remove the phone for the upcoming conversation, grabbed the phone and slipped it into his pocket. He wanted the teen to be able to discuss her feelings face to face rather than competing with her burying her emotions in the phone with whomever she was texting. It did not take long for our little Mae Mae to rat Ron out by saying, "Hey! He likes your phone!" She was urgently pointing her finger at his pocket and drawing attention to the missing phone. Her preschool antics truly broke all the tension in the room and gave everyone a good laugh! The teen was able to crack a smile too and proceed with telling us about her day.

We are also aware of technoference. This is a concept that was originally developed to describe parents' feelings when children avoid interacting with them (both on purpose and incidentally) because of the constant barrage of stimulation from the media. Anymore though, technoference also refers to the idea of children being ignored by their parents for the same reasons. There are youngsters who know their parents mostly with a phone glued to their face.

Several studies done over the past decade have reviewed the effects of heavy Internet use and excessive video gaming, which suggest a reduction of gray matter in the brain and which has actually generated its own term called digital dementia.[9] What a frightening thought if this is found to be true! This is why we often engage the children in cognitive activities like large puzzles that promote thought processing. I saw a comic the other day where a man is standing at a beautiful gate, surrounded by clouds, talking to an angel. The angel glances at his scroll and states, "Says here you *did* have a pretty great life but were looking down at your phone and missed it."

Parents want preteens and teens to start internalizing the understanding of how prevalent media usage should or should not be in their lives. For teens who cannot see any value in setting their own limits, we must do more with natural consequences and removal of privileges. That is a lot more work. We emphasize heavily that whenever teens can have a say in helping to set their own limitations, the follow-through on their part will go better, and our level of trust in them will be stronger. Our hope is to guide them to understand why making good decisions benefits their health and well-being.

There are parents who are satisfied with the phone being the primary babysitter to their child, but this has consequences later, ranging from low language development skills, decreased comfort with social skills, secrecy, isolation, and more. As Mother Teresa once said, "What do you do in secret? Doing things in secret, hiding, these things are the beginning of lying."[10] While it is understandable that children want to be on their phones more often, if you the parent do not want to monitor it, then I would say that less time with phones and social media is better. Foster mom friend Jayne sent me a quote that said, "Give your kids social media when you want their childhood to end." I don't disagree.

Back to seventeen-year-old Theo who, despite having a callused thick outer layer, deep down was really delightful. He was funny, loved old movies, and played soccer well. He never once brought up not having a cell phone; he just said his current foster mom simply did not allow them in her home. It gave me a renewed respect for this lady who was old school in her beliefs and was on to something good, I think. Cell phones take a lot of time away from family interaction and subdue children's tendencies to show and share their feelings with caring adults. Overused, it is a wedge that cuts into healthy family time.

Sixteen-year-old Maxine chose not to follow our cell phone policy. It was too different from the 24/7 access to her phone she was used to at home with her mother. Thankfully, she was able to go into a relative kinship placement to her aunt's home within a few days of placement here, so we chose not to take on this battle. The trouble is I still see what she posts online, and it is not good. Her brother, whom we still see, tells me the aunt sees it too but "can't control her." A year later she has gone through a half dozen kinship placements and still has not found a stable home. My guess is she will age out of the foster-care system first and continue with her abusive, dominating, and bullying behaviors. The lesson here is that we cannot help every person whom we meet; we just try our best where we can.

SELF-DISCIPLINE

In our situation, we do not deal with driving issues often because most children in foster care do not drive, and our biological children are all adults. Our friend Renee uses a parental monitoring app that she likes because it tells her where her teens are, how fast they drive, and if they used their phones during the drive time. To ensure safety, attentive parents should use technology safeguards and boundaries to set limits on phone usage while driving. Where we can place more decision-making and trust in the child, we do, but for some teens that more mature thinking can be a long time coming.

Allowing teenagers to drive is all about trusting their decision-making skills. If the teen has shown they are trustworthy in small matters, we feel more confident letting go of the reins and trusting them in bigger matters. Children who have suffered many traumas are usually less mature, and good decision-making skills can be delayed. If our trust is ever broken with the teen, we would not hesitate to take away the car keys for a period of time or have them ride the bus to school as a natural consequence until the trust was restored.

On the same note, our advice to our teens is not to get into expendable daily rituals like store-bought specialty coffees, or even *try* smoking, vaping, drugs, or alcohol because they might just like it. Huge health concerns aside, those purchases will change the trajectory of their lives financially. We try to teach the children that while one day they may have adequate money to indulge in extra treats, fast-food outings, and shopping trips to the mall, they may want to consider saving their earned money instead. Ron being in finance explains to them that putting a little money aside each month will make a big difference in having the ability to purchase a car or house in the future.

Regarding peer pressure, we simply state the obvious. Allowing someone else to influence the children's decisions usually will not go well and could have life-or-death consequences. Every generation faces this. We ask them to choose what they know to be right and wrong, not what is popular. Doing so shows emotional intelligence, self-control, and strength. Having confidence in themselves and making good decisions early in their lives will control the direction of life.

Keeping a close eye out for illegal (and legal) drug usage is a parent's job too. Educate yourself with a formal class taught by law enforcement. They keep up to date on the latest information and are worth every bit of effort it takes to get there. I have taken drug-awareness training several times and I learn hundreds of new facts every time I go, even if it had only been a year since my last class. Since there is so much insidious behavior associated with using, go and learn this information from a professional. There is no substitute. It's like cancer; the earlier you catch a problem and stop turning a blind eye to the symptoms, the greater the chance of recovery.

Self-regulation in polite society is not too much to ask and is a crucial insight that children will draw on from the rest of their lives, especially when taught early on. I know some twelve-year-olds who are better decision-makers than some twenty-year-olds. Teaching youth how far-reaching decisions today can affect their every tomorrow matters.

EXTRACURRICULAR ACTIVITIES

We support finding every child an activity to participate in. Having an activity gives children a reason to work at being proficient at something, a place to fit in with peers, and is beneficial for their minds and bodies. We enjoy going to their meets, games, and performances. We wave around a homemade sign or take a flower to congratulate them. Taking a picture is always involved to remember the positive experience, and it shows the children they are worthy of our time and effort.

Extracurricular activities and hobbies reduce stress and help important friendships develop for children. Allowing children to feel that they are going to be okay at your home means normalizing their days as much as possible and helping them find places to fit in. The "new kid" identity is one that most children are not used to and do not want. Extracurricular activities can give children a sense of normalcy, friends to interact with, and a schedule to follow.

Our hope is also that children are less likely to get into trouble when they are busy. Helping children find comfort in sports, crafts, or collections gives them something to look forward to each day instead of sitting around complaining that there is nothing to do. Children build their foundation with experiences; this includes activities with their peers. These things all help a child mature socially, emotionally, and physically. When children are young, their guiding voice is their parent; as they age, a teen's guiding voice is friends and media, so we offer choices of carefully selected activities to combat this. We support the child's interest and talent, especially the ones that have the best chance of being a positive influence on them.

We gradually introduce a new hobby, club, or sports team. We have the children meet the coaches or leaders ahead of time and then encourage them to ease into friendships and structured activities. We prepare them for what we think will happen and answer their questions. Ron uses his great coaching skills to teach the children beginning sports skills and about plays and strategies. Having a rudimentary understanding of the game ahead of time helps the children catch up to their peers who may have been playing the game for years.

We never use extracurricular activities or hobby interests as consequences to be removed as a discipline because these types of activities should not be taken away from children. Nor should they be something that they only attend sporadically. Children should know that when they join a group or club, they will attend the meeting, practices, and games as scheduled. We remove privileges elsewhere when needed.

Focusing on being a member of a club or part of a sports team helps a child focus on a group skill and instills a sense of belonging. Activities that center around their talents bring out the best in the child. Children can do a couple of different activities until they find a place that fits their personality and skill.

Maurice was a fantastic little athlete even at age four. He could sink a basketball into the hoop, dribble easily between his legs without looking, and could catch any ball thrown at him. He was so fun to watch and naturally drew the attention of others. He also expressed an interest in baseball, so we signed him up for the local t-ball team to give him a place to hone his skills and meet other little boys his age. He loved having big foster brother Matthew to practice with and beamed with pride as all his siblings—biological and foster— watched him play ball. Years later, we still catch a game of his on occasion.

Several of our high school teens felt a lot of pride participating in sports teams. Donte played baseball, Anna played basketball, and Chris played football. Denny joined the swim team and Lee joined the marching band. The set practice schedule of these extracurricular activities is not always easy to follow and takes time to adjust to and the guts not to quit. But, having a place to go and forming relationships with coaches and peers is usually enough draw to entice them to stick out the commitment.

Buck needed an outlet for all his energy after school. We have established great relationships with a few area coaches who are more than happy to have our foster children join in on their practices when they are in our home, if even for just a few weeks. Coach W would swing by our house a few days a week to pick up Buck on his way to practice. Buck was ecstatic to be included on a team and improved his skills too. When he comes back for visits, he always asks about Coach W and the boys and if we remember how he was part of the team. I know this will always be a cherished memory for him.

One piece of advice I heard years ago was to avoid the tempting trap parents can fall into regarding needing to make all childhood activities about future resume building. For logistical reasons, my friend Kris and her husband James, adoptive parents of nine, had to limit how many activities their children could participate in. She told me that they would still be good at sports even if they didn't start playing until middle school, when organized sports are offered through the school. She was right. Every time we go to see one of her children participate in their special activity, they are fantastic at it. Maybe this is because the children's joints and muscles aren't full of injuries already from starting training too young. Or maybe it's because they are not already burnt out from demanding practice schedules at an early age. Regardless, now that they are in middle school, they really are something to watch!

Not all extracurriculars must be team related. Hobbies are a great activity too. We are big fans of working puzzles with the children because they all have a different approach on the best way to work it. Edges or middle first is a friendly debated topic in our home. Four-year-old Tre was delayed in both his speech and social skill development when he arrived at our home, but he did show a mild interest in puzzles. Ron's mother, a dedicated educator, taught us years ago that an early interest in puzzles can be an indicator of children who will thrive in math and science skills.

As the months went by, family members started picking up additional puzzles at stores and garage sales because we could not keep up with his interest in them. Family members would get down on the floor to work puzzles with him and prompt more conversation, speech, and adult interaction time. Tre, who on the day we received the original placement call was described as having autistic tendencies, definitely no longer fits that description. As he approaches his teen years, his engineering-type brain is getting even brighter.

Another hobby enthusiast, Kym, was a big fan of playing all games, which was good because she lived with us the year we had seven foster children in our home. She wanted to avoid any kind of conflict because it seemed to be a trigger to her past. When Ron would hear an argument brewing in the playroom or see someone being left out, he called everyone over to investigate. Usually the issue was boredom, so another activity was started. Thankfully Ron liked playing games too, so Kym would always volunteer to participate in a new game. Specifically, Kym loved playing Old Maid. To keep things exciting and to keep Kym's attention, Ron would try to make her pick the Old Maid card by sticking that card out further than the others. Bending the conventional rules of the game always ended with a lot of laughs. It was an ongoing silly tactic between the two of them that gave Kym a break from the others when they were bothering her.

Being highly proficient at an activity is often a precursor to a lifelong hobby or even a job skill. Our foster daughter Autumn was a beautiful artist. For her, art was an emotional escape. When she could not express herself verbally, she drew. When she was sad, she drew. To gain respect at school, she drew. She ended up designing the cover of a book in a contest, and after that she and her skills became well recognized amongst her peers. There is no doubt she will go into a vocation where her artistic talents will be useful. I hope to see one of her amazing drawings on a billboard or in an art museum someday.

TEACHING LIFE SKILLS

There are opportunities to learn simple life skills in every situation. Children's levels of common sense vary exponentially based on their experiences. So many children do not know simple skills. Household skills like cooking, laundry, gardening, and simple repairs can be taught in an age-appropriate way to any child older than a tot. We garden together, pull weeds along the way, harvest, and talk about the health benefits of growing our own food and eating clean when possible. We share our produce with our neighbors.

Showing the proper use of simple tools such as a hammer, screwdriver, or drill for older children is appropriate. Miguel was old enough to learn to hang shelves properly by using a stud finder, drill, wall anchors, and a level. He considered himself an expert by the time he hung the third shelf. Cheyenne wanted to move her bedroom furniture around, so she learned to measure where the new location of the pieces would fit, how to use a wrench to unscrew tightened bolts, and how to correctly reassemble the room. We always teach age-appropriate first aid too, especially when working with tools.

Educating children with general knowledge tidbits is important because it provides the opportunity for a conversation with an adult and sparks interest in a new topic. The sun rises in the east and sets in the west helps them understand that they will always be able to tell which direction they are going. We discuss extreme weather conditions, so they know to stay off an elevated land mass when severe storms or lightning is occurring and when to seek shelter. We practice where to meet in case of a fire or a tornado.

We talk about conversions such as two halves equal a whole, four quarters equal a dollar, and how to tie shoes. We sing songs about ABCs, Bible verses, telling time, and the water cycle. Safety issues like good hand washing, not getting too close to the hot stove, proper use of a helmet, and not bothering dogs when they are eating are always reviewed. We instruct on hygiene practices like zippered dust mite covers for all mattresses and box springs and explain why white linens are easiest to bleach. We play act the Safety Town chant—stop, drop, and roll—for clothing on fire. We explain how to crawl out of a smoky room and what to do if they find a gun (Stop. Don't Touch. Leave the Area. Tell an Adult!).

For older children, we will discuss how to calculate 10% of a restaurant or salon bill. To promote kindness to others, we teach them to double the amount for a tip of excellent service. We practice calculating the correct change needed back from a purchase. Oh, my goodness, do we practice that! We talk about how to shop with coupons, how to figure out a sale, and how to analyze what is needed versus what is wanted. Almost everyone learns to sew on a button and how to manage a simple hem. They learn to handwrite thank-you cards. We explain simple financial ideas like how a debit account differs from a savings account and the advantages and disadvantages between renting or buying a home and leasing or buying a vehicle.

Most importantly, we want to teach our children that there is joy in the process of learning life skills and that projects do not always have to be dreaded. If we can teach our children to enjoy and take pride in their work, they will come to appreciate their God-given talents. We encourage children to form a career goal centered around their talents. A parent instills confidence and teaches as many skills as possible for children to overcome their past traumas and have the best chance to flourish.

WHEN CHILDREN BECOME ADULTS

Matthew and I use a term that we have labeled as "Mom and Matthew moments." This is a rendition of what used to be "Mom and Matthew Mondays," which was our quality time together when he was in high school, and I had a standing babysitter for any foster children we might have in the house at that time. Every Monday evening was our set time for us—and Dad when his schedule allowed—to go out to dinner. These were the years our three daughters were away at college and starting their independent adult lives and we were all missing them.

As the years flew by and he headed off to college too, our quality time together changed from days to moments. There are always mixed emotions in parenting—*sad to see them go and happy to see them leave* type of feeling. Whether it is off to college, time for foster children to leave, or when a significant change in family dynamic occurs, we are grateful for our time together and know that it will be okay because it's just another chapter in life. We appreciate what we have today and take time to prepare things to look forward to in the future to help ourselves transition. We train our brain toward peace and gratitude. As my dad always says about growing old, "It's better than the alternative."

CHAPTER 12: COMMUNITY ACTION

Instilling a sense of community in a child is crucial. Spending time within their local community to do their part in making it better is another way to teach children to think outside themselves. Thankfully, there are so many wonderful people who desire this for our next generation too. We surround our children with adults who encourage social responsibility in hopes the children will come to know this as an important part of their life as well.

GET INVOLVED

Ron and I believe that volunteer work encourages children to see the world around them from a different perspective. There are few activities better than volunteering that help us see firsthand that life is better for ourselves than we often think. Even children can find healing growth by doing something kind for another person. Great experiences come from these opportunities.

Ron rings the bell for the Salvation Army and takes the children in our home, young and old, every once in a while. It is a powerful lesson about recognizing that others have genuine needs too. Many groups of children, including our own, have donned Santa hats and taken a turn ringing the bell for the Salvation Army kettle drive. When numerous littles all go on one day, we make sure everyone has their own set of jingle bells to ring.

I think volunteering helps with lessening the "woe is me" phenomenon, fosters empathy toward others, and makes us less self-centered. Besides helping us to feel good, volunteering is powerful because the hormones our body releases improve our mood and fight stress. Serving others takes our mind off ourselves and focuses it on someone else. Plus it helps children learn new skills and make new friends. These feelings promote a sense of belonging to a community and help build the child's self-esteem. Of course, the best scenario is when a parent volunteers with the child.

There are other important aspects of the community that we stress. When children come into foster care, the ideal goal for the agency is to place children in their own neighborhood, school, and faith community, if possible. If this is impossible, then we make arrangements to attend events in their home community together with them as a means of keeping community connections as strong as possible.

Tre, Ron, and I recently went to a community event in the area that Tre used to live in before he came into foster care. It was a wonderful day filled with fellowship, boys running around playing, and eating hot dogs and ice cream. We took Andie to a community donation drive in her neighborhood where she helped organize toys and clothes to be passed out to other children. She was so proud to help, and she enjoyed seeing some of her classmates from her old school as they came through.

As children mature and become better able to handle themselves publicly, we encourage increased time spent out in the community because it helps children put their personal time, talent, and treasure to good use. We want to see children helping others outside of themselves and build their character. If we teach children to volunteer in their younger years, having a heart of service will come more naturally to them in adulthood. Ideally, great positivity will come from these diverse social experiences, creating lasting memories that will impact their lives for the better.

BABYSITTERS

Having a trusted babysitter for a house full of children is an absolute Godsend. In the foster-care world, a babysitter would be referred to as an alternative caregiver. In essence, they are community members who volunteer as "approved" babysitters for us, which is an immense help! Sometimes these helpers make the difference in us being able to keep the placement of a child intact versus it falling through from sustained stress that we can no longer handle. Babysitters also have the same effect in giving a family a needed break for a dinner out or the opportunity to get errands run quickly without toting the children in and out of stores.

Alternative caregivers are *the* essential support beam for adults. Relatives and friends who volunteer their services so we parents can take a day off play an important role in helping us succeed as parents. Quite frankly, if you know a family who is struggling, step in to intervene and offer to help. This may actually prevent negative situations from escalating or prevent the removal of their children. With hundreds of thousands of children in foster care in the United States, the need for people to get involved truly exists.[11] It is fashionable to talk about helping others. It's another thing to step in and do it. Our son Matthew once said, "What I like about foster care is that we are actually doing something to help others instead of just talking about it."

Alternative caregivers can further enrich our foster children's lives by doing other things with them that we are unable to do. One summer day Rose, our teen foster daughter, went on a daytime boating excursion on Lake Erie with our alternative caregivers. This in combination with her interest in the armed services prompted a fact-finding search on the

US Coast Guard. What a wonderful period of enlightenment for her! Inspiration can come from anywhere. All these small steps, sometimes brought to light by an alternative caregiver, lead to fresh knowledge, growing confidence, and stability for the child.

After spending that day with my dad learning about installing shelves, Miguel, now feeling proud of his new knowledge and skills, took it upon himself to disassemble and reassemble several beds that needed arranged that very day for a new set of children coming to our foster home later in the afternoon. He gathered the information from me about which child was going in what room and developed a plan. He now knew the difference between a screw bit and a drill bit and how to use them both. Soon he was my fix-it guy around the house with other projects and wanted any jobs requiring tools reserved for him. He had a generous personality by nature, so I can easily see why he enjoyed helping.

My stance has always been that there need to be four or five support families who stand behind each home with children. Whether this support is from family members, neighbors, babysitters, or alternative caregivers, most everyone needs some level of assistance while raising children, especially those children who have significant trauma in their backgrounds. Trauma parenting is not the same as parenting normal-needs children. Some days having a friend stand behind me and hold my head above water is all that gets me through.

One family in our community took a special liking to our young foster son Davy. They babysat for us when we needed help, took him out for an ice cream cone every now and again, showed up at his baseball practice as a surprise, and greeted him with a high five after church each Sunday. To this day, it is a special memory of a kind family who took time out of their busy schedule to make this five-year-old feel important.

As a bit of an unusual parenting tip, I have learned to schedule what I call "ghost babysitters." I ask my alternative caregivers to keep a certain important date open just in case I would have a foster child that day. One weekend, we had two important events planned: an academic ceremony on Friday and a charity event on Saturday. While we had no foster children at that time, we planned in case we did get a fostering call. We had two different stand-by babysitters set up for that weekend, one on each night, as a precaution. While we didn't end up with any children that particular weekend, these people are always so dear to understand our atypical circumstances and cheerfully pencil us onto their calendar in case we have a last-minute need.

As a community member, you can be part of the ongoing support of a family. Selflessly sharing adult time, treasure, and talent allows children to expand their experiences and maybe promotes development of a skill in the time they are with you. These special outings are an effort to plan and implement, but they offer a tired parent time to slow down and rest. In the case of stress or trauma, these special days can replace bad memories and stories with good ones.

Every positive adult interaction, whether it be with a parent, a coach, or a neighbor, helps shape the story of a child's life and gives them increased opportunities to thrive. In a time when generational help from extended family is not always available and burnout is prevalent when caring for children, alternative childcare is a necessary factor in our demanding society. For thriving societies to continue, we must step up and take the job to raise the next generation together.

MENTORING

Mentors are knowledgeable individuals who help parents raise children, often in a more formal way. Mentoring helps increase maturity and growth in children because they are processing words and instructions in a different setting with another adult. These happenings, which are likely different from their normal everyday routine, help their development.

Mentors generously pitch in to share their unique knowledge of a topic with activities for the children to participate in and provide new knowledge to draw on in the future. For traumatized children, mentors and parents, when well matched, help combat the setbacks from a lack of diverse positive experiences in their lifetimes. For regular-needs children, it is an opportunity for further growth. Afterall, not everyone knows how to budget, change a tire, or woodwork. We use mentoring experiences to pass information and skills from one generation to the next. Experiences help children move on and grow up.

When we would visit my mom in Florida, she was always teaching our children the different names of flowers. She loved nature and plants, and she wanted to pass this on to her grandchildren too. It was years after her passing that I found out that she gave them a dollar for every plant they named correctly, or incorrectly for that matter. My children still fondly remember the flowers Nana taught them and can still name them today.

Our two young foster children Lyndsey and Jacob had little stimulation or life experiences outside of their rundown home. They lacked basic hygiene understanding, physical coordination due to malnutrition, and their speech was almost nonexistent. Thankfully, a friend with a farm had these children out to visit frequently where they could run around, play with chickens and dogs, and learn to fish. They needed all sorts of stimulation and interaction and found that on the farm!

Parents work to provide the basics, like proper supervision, good nutrition, and a stable home. Expanding further, we want to layer children with other forms of support through teachers, therapists, and mentors. Other fun activities that Lyndsey and Jacob enjoyed were library reading hour, preschool science center day, creative movement dance class, Bible school, and baking cookies with Meemaw. These activities stimulated their social, emotional, educational, and physical development in ways that would be different than if they had all their experiences every day with the same person.

A set of five school-aged siblings rarely traveled out of their neighborhood before coming into foster care. One day, we took them on an adventure and traveled north to see the water and beach of Lake Erie; another day we took them several hours south and deep into Amish Country. They had no idea that either of these places existed and told us they had never seen a live cow or horse before! We had taken sketchbooks along because they all had great natural artistic talent. They chronicled their day with various drawings of their experiences; these were then placed in their memory books along with the photos from the day. They talked about these adventures the entire year they lived here with us, like they had traveled the world or something. The experiences made a big impression.

Some of our older children experienced days with mentor friends who took them out on excursions like roller skating, a zoo day, and an afternoon at a friend's nail and hair salon. We found that the more the children got out of the house, the more positive changes we saw in their behaviors. They had activities to look forward to, gained new experiences, and had memories to talk about. We found them to be less bored and mopey and saw decreases in their behavioral antics.

Lots of adults still have room in their hearts and homes for some child interaction time. Mentoring has long been known as an effective treatment for feelings of loneliness or sadness that empty nesters and retirees can have. Elders who pass along stories, traditions, and knowledge to the younger generation are sharing invaluable life lessons. My father helped twelve-year-old Sergeant repair, sand, stain, and rehang the oak door he damaged one day at our home. It would have taken far less time and effort for Dad to do the repair himself, but the grandfatherly time spent teaching the mischievous teen a useful repair skill was the bigger gift. Like most parents, we deeply appreciate those altruistic mentors who have stepped forward to assist us in our attempts to navigate childhood challenges and pass along their valuable knowledge.

Our background and circumstances influence who we are, but we are responsible for who we become. Parents and mentors setting up time to spend with children gives them positive memories to hold and delightful stories to tell. Healing starts by filling the gaps from trauma, illness, or other adversities with optimism, goals, and hope. Caring adults guide children away from being forever defined by the negative events in their lives and build momentum for brighter days ahead.

HOLIDAYS

Holidays in blended families require creative scheduling. Not overplanning helps maintain sanity. However, carefully planned holiday gatherings still produce unfamiliar routines and oftentimes unwanted stimulation and memories for children. Some children may be sad while still adjusting to being away from their own family, while everyone else in the room is overjoyed. You can imagine the disappointment of the child who came to our foster home on Christmas Eve. Realistically, we cannot alter every situation to benefit the child's feelings, but we can try our best to prepare them for what will happen ahead of time.

If age appropriate, we ask the children what they are expecting the holiday might bring or if they would like to tell us how their family celebrates. We try to incorporate into our day things that seem especially meaningful to them. Next, we let them know our usual holiday happenings and keep an eye on how the events of the day unwind so we can intervene if something becomes upsetting. Our goal is to help the child feel included but not overwhelmed. Likewise, we prepare our extended family members for the foster children by giving them tips and tricks about the child to help everyone feel comfortable and safe.

We encourage our family to provide a calm greeting rather than smothering the children with well wishes. Sometimes new children just need a couple of minutes in the background to get their bearings. When we arrive at a new place, we give the children a quick tour of their surroundings, including where the bathroom is. We keep hugs or other forms of affection light and polite. We remain sensitive to the conversations around the child, keeping chats lighthearted and not too serious, and are conscientious that alcohol could be triggering for some children. We then depart before they are overly tired and behaviors begin to fade.

Mother's Day and Father's Day festivities can bring especially poignant feelings for children and families. With foster children, we set up phone conversations when appropriate, draw pictures, and write letters to be sent to the families ahead of the holiday. Oftentimes, we enlarge a family photo of the children and their parents and place it in a crafting frame, which we let children color or paint. We send the gift to their family visit a week ahead of the holiday so the mother and/or father has the gift to open on the actual Mother's or Father's Day. Since we openly pray with our children about their families, always blessing their parents and siblings, they know that we know how important the day is as we pray for their mommies and daddies, brothers and sisters, and any helper mommies and daddies they have had along the way.

We know of a family where the four siblings are being raised by three different relatives. One child lives with the grandmother, another with an aunt, and two with the biological father. While it may not be ideal for the children to be split up, the children are with their family and do get to see their siblings on major holidays. I spoke to their mom on the phone a couple of years after this arrangement was decided by the court system, and she stated that she drives up a couple times a year from the south to keep in touch with her children also.

Our stoic Miguel normally did not show much emotion. The day he came into care, I asked him about his family traditions for Christmas, which had been the week before. As I looked in the rearview mirror of my car, I saw him brush a tear aside when he said they had never celebrated a Christmas, even though they believed in the holiday. That weekend, together with him and his sister, we planned a late Christmas celebration. We dressed in holiday clothes, made a festive meal, sang carols, and got them a few gifts. We also included several relatives who brought small gifts. We took photos of the festivities so the children could remember that they too got to celebrate Christmas that year.

Over the years, we have developed a rotation system in our home, especially with the larger holidays, to keep the bedlam to a minimum. At family get-togethers, gift giving may end up being overwhelming for both children and adults, so we often let all the little ones open their gifts first. They get to make a big mess and have lots of loud fun.

We then start round two with the adult members of the family doing the slow and deliberate unwrap while the little ones enjoy their new gifts. The speedsters have been given the chance to release all their pent-up energy while still letting the other family members, who like to savor the moment, have their quiet celebration too. Both years that we had ten children in the house we did three rounds: the tots, the teens, and then the adults. While this situation may be a bit unusual, each set of family members felt noticed and excited during the day's festivities.

DAYCARE

A good daycare center can be invaluable to parents for several reasons. Parents who have jobs that require them to work outside the home will likely use a daycare center. In some instances, stay-at-home caregivers may want to consider doing the same, even if only on occasion. While this may not be needed for someone raising their own child, a child with high needs could benefit from having this experience.

Though daycare fees are hefty and the work of setting up the service is tedious, I still think it is worth the effort. The centers have many regulations they are obligated to follow. To expedite the process, we keep copies of daycare centers' mandatory forms in our home and take them to the initial doctor exam the very first week the child is placed in our home. We get medical clearance forms done with every youngster even if we are not sure we are going to use daycare.

We will also try to anticipate if the child needs medical documentation for school, sports teams, or after-school activities. I try my best to acquire this paperwork ahead of the doctor appointment to make the most of the visit and to not have to drag the children to countless appointments later. We find it easier to already have forms filled out and ready than get the forms sent, completed, and returned later. This creates fewer emails and headaches.

One good reason to have reliable daycare staff to fall back on is that parents constantly put their own medical needs last, and having a routinely scheduled time with childcare can help discourage that practice. Not having daytime babysitters is one less reason to skip that dental cleaning. Quite frankly, some days parents just need a break to catch up on their own work and to have a day to mentally reset. Daycare is an exciting outing for the child and a golden opportunity for self-care for the adult.

The daycare setting is also very useful in giving the children chances to socialize with their peers and work on cooperation skills. Experienced staff are skilled at child behaviors and will reinforce your chosen parenting techniques if it is communicated to them. Our five preschool brothers benefited from daycare a great deal since they did not spend a lot of time outside of their apartment before coming into foster care. They benefited from peer interaction, loved the abundance of toys, took a few steps in the direction of cooperative play, and got to have fun with friends doing all the great activities daycare provides. The daycare staff also did a cursory assessment of their educational needs, which prompted me to seek further evaluations from our local school system. They learned to follow the teacher's rules and take direction from another adult, all while allowing some needed down time for Ron and me.

INDIVIDUALIZED EDUCATION PLANS

All schools offer Individualized Education Plans to support children according to their individualized academic and behavioral needs and abilities. Specifically, an IEP is a process where several types of academic and psychological evaluations are given to a child at school to assess their academic and social needs. A combination of academic aptitude, social skills, and emotional maturity will be assessed. Not all children need an IEP for school success, but traumatized children have a higher likelihood of having this need because of their history.

While only some children will qualify for an IEP, I recommend that anyone having big behavioral issues with their child consider investigating the possible need for one. The IEP process has many steps to get one set up, but it is totally worth the effort! The importance lies in the fact that should the child qualify for this school program, the documentation of an IEP will follow the child no matter which school they are placed in or where they are living for the next several years.

It can be somewhat confusing to know whether the child's academic needs or behaviors are severe enough to need an IEP. I often ask our adult daughter Katherine, who is a schoolteacher, to give me an initial opinion. Between her years of teaching experience and being a biological child who was raised alongside many different foster siblings herself, she has a unique perspective to understand which children may need intervention. My best advice to others is to find a teacher, counselor, or classroom aide who seems to have a connection with the child in question and ask them for their opinion regarding whether the child seems to be on target with peers, behaviorally and academically. Through the years, I have found this to be incredibly helpful.

Astonishingly enough, I have been told that teachers cannot necessarily bring up school issues they suspect but instead often have to wait for a parent to ask them about it first. For the longest time, I did not know that. After taking care of so many different children, sometimes it's hard to remember what a normal developing child looks and acts like. Most teachers are experts and can give good guidance one way or the other.

Once the decision has been made that a formal evaluation of the child is needed, a doctor's order is required to initiate the assessment process. Tests will then be administered and analyzed. The assessors will weigh in with their observations and recommendations, determined by the test scores, for a plan of action to support the child's school needs. When the child returns to their home or moves on to a kinship or adoptive placement, and a school change is necessary, the new teachers and staff can pick up the accommodations and modifications as stated in the IEP without missing a beat. It is also an emotional safety net, in my opinion, with more eyes on the child when they leave my home. Having a physical, occupational, or speech therapist as well as other school staff routinely interacting with the child all adds up to extra, keen adult eyes keeping watch over them.

We had a large sibling group of six where every child needed IEP evaluations. It literally took an entire school year to get that one task accomplished because there are so many steps in starting the process and seeing it through to completion for each child. This included teacher evaluations, formal academic testing, counseling sessions, pediatrician appointments, and forms galore to fill out. On the day the children were returned to their grandmother, the last child's IEP meeting had literally just finished hours before the move.

For a qualifying child or a teen, initiating services through a formal IEP assessment is one of the absolute best interventions you can pursue to help them down the road. Parents who are dedicated to getting evaluations made, assessments done, followed-through meetings scheduled, and the actual help initiated are helping significantly to further the child's education and likely their quality of life.

CHAPTER 13: FINAL THOUGHTS

There are many ideas I have kept in my back pocket as the years of parenting have gone on, but the best advice I can give overall is to lovingly raise the child you are parenting with the mindset of accentuating their positive behaviors and abilities and downplaying the negatives as much as possible. All children are good and are a gift from God, and so are the amazing parents who are trying to give them a strong foundation and prepare them for life ahead.

ROOKIE MISTAKES

Rarely a day goes by when I don't scold myself with my go-to statement, "Ahh, Kathleen, that was a rookie mistake!"

Even though I have been involved with children from the child welfare system for more than three decades, I continue to learn every day. I would like to share a few of the big mistakes I have learned along the way in hopes of preventing someone else from making them. Some of these are foster-care related, but adjust the details and you may still find them useful in other settings.

I now know to double-check placement information when a call comes in to take children into our home. I no longer accept the initial stated age of the child as absolute unless I ask for the child's birthday and verify their age for myself. Our very first little girl placed with us all those years ago who was supposed to be five years old really turned out to be barely two. Then we had Baby Anne, who was supposedly five pounds at birth, but when they brought her to our home, she was five pounds at six months—just then leaving the hospital from her birth six months earlier. Born at twenty-four weeks gestation, she weighed only 1.2 pounds! And then, there was the teen girl of exceptional size who opened the car door and tried to jump out of my moving car. With all my might, I reached out and pulled her back in. I discern that initial placement call much more carefully now. Verifying correct ages and asking if the child is exceptionally big or exceptionally small have become routine so I can be better prepared.

In recent years, the children's services agency that we foster through has provided a placement packet when the child comes to our home. It consists of a pair of pajamas, a new set of weather-appropriate clothes, a pair of underpants/socks, and a toothbrush set. This is a lovely gesture, but so many times the sizes aren't even close to being useful. When nine-year-old Perry came to our home, he was underweight at thirty-six pounds. He fit in a boy's size six clothing and was delivered to us with a "medium pack." Unfortunately, it was a men's medium, and the sweatpants alone were longer than his entire height. When taking a child in, I ask the worker to double-check this emergency pack before they head to my house so the items are actually useful, especially since so many children arrive into foster care unexpectedly and late at night.

Sometimes I forget to brace myself for that "anything can happen phenomenon." Children's emotions can catch us off guard, especially when comments or concerns come up so unexpectedly. Keeping this in mind, I remember when Lia yelled out that she was being choked when I lifted her chin to show her how to look an adult in the eye. Her older brother sitting right next to her said, "What are you talking about? She didn't choke you. Seriously Lia, you are so dramatic!"

In a different incident with Lia, the nurse at the doctor's office wanted to know if she needed to get an attorney when bloodcurdling screams came from Lia's shouting "You're killing me! You're killing me! You're killing me!" as the blood pressure cuff inflated. The sweet nurse was in tears because children in the lobby heard this and became upset too. All I could do was apologize profusely to her and assure her she didn't need legal representation. Still, these antics are hurtful, especially when the real story is that the difficult children were really receiving excellent care.

I often hear people quitting or retiring from foster caregiving say it wasn't what they were expecting; I always think to myself *Neither is parenting or life, for that matter.* Successful parenting is not about being perfect or better than anyone else but about learning, growing, and evolving in parenting skills all in the hopes of raising safe and responsible children. We learn to adjust, appreciate small moments of success, and get up and try again the next day. We often send texts to other parents wishing them an "even" day. Parents get what that means. Not all days in life are a photo op. Behind the scenes we cry, we have grit, we adjust, and we cope.

ENDLESS ACCESSORIES

We are still coming up with novel parenting ideas every day because each child placement brings new aspects of care that we have not experienced before. We try to see from the child's perspective, both literally and figuratively. We set up our house to promote both independence and responsibility. For example, we use hooks that are at a child's height as a simple means to keep jackets and coats hung up independently by the child. Even toddlers are capable and willing to use them. We have a wall in our laundry room with twenty-five hooks conveniently placed for school backpacks, diaper bags, library totes, and sports equipment. These hooks prevent us from ever having to search the house for a ballet shoe, a baseball glove, or a library book and allow us to keep a bag packed week to week for a designated activity.

One winter, we had four children under five, so we placed a clothesline across from our laundry room and used clothes pins to hang all the hats and gloves there. This idea was especially helpful because most of the items were wet when we took them off the children either from snow play or drooling mouths, and this allowed them to dry out in the fresh air instead of being stacked on top of each other somewhere. We could see all the sizes of hats and gloves at a glance, which allowed us to do a quick grab and go as we walked out the door.

COLOR CODING

Another tried-and-true hint is adopting a color-coding system. This cuts down on confusion. When a child comes into our home, we allow them to choose a colorful plate set to be their own. From that point on, meals are always served with that dish set. We offer many colors and character sets too. This is also helpful when preparing plates for the child who doesn't want mayonnaise on their sandwich or the one who has an allergy to peanut butter. I always know whose plate is whose.

In the case of twins, I always imagine one twin as the oldest and mark their item in a darker color. Darker because older kids typically like blues and greens as their favorite color and younger children like pinks. In the case of medications, I give a prescribed dose to the "blue" twin first and the "pink" twin second, assuming of course that they are both on it. I have the older child go first at checkups too. The idea of thinking of one twin as the older one cuts back on confusion as I wonder which child did what. Trust me, after parenting seven sets of twins and several sets of "Irish twins" (siblings born in the same calendar year and who are practically twins), it is an excellent way to keep the children straight and the medications going into the right mouth.

One clever mom color coded her children because she had identical twin girls placed with her. She chose to put a red item in Ronna's hair every day (either a clip, headband, or a bow). Donna always wore another color besides red. The children could be readily identified and called by the correct name every time by anyone who knew the secret identifying code: red for Ronna. This was a brilliant strategy because I have never seen any twins who looked as much alike as they did!

Color coding can be a safety trick as well. When our four children were young, we had matching color swim sets to use at the local swimming lake. The girls had matching bows in neon bright colors: green, yellow, and orange. Our son had matching goggles and swim trunks in the same color. They were easy to spot in the lake and the lifeguards frequently commented on how they knew exactly when our family arrived for the day because our children were so easily visible. The lifeguards got so accustomed to watching four matching swimmers that it got to the point that if one of our children was not present to swim that day, we would report the information to the guard stand to prevent worry.

DOCUMENTING CHILDHOOD

The building of a child's self-esteem is the main reason we embrace the idea of a memory or scrapbook. I recommend some form of this for all children. We started documenting our children's lives on the day they were born in the hopes of giving them photos and videos to look back on. In the foster-care world, this is called a "lifebook." The purpose of a lifebook is to give the child an accurate understanding of how their time in foster care was spent.

This scrapbook of sorts serves as a timeline history document and source of information for the child and their family. Every child gets a lifebook when they are placed with us, whether for two days or two years. We use a two-inch binder to house the lifebook to keep the project minimally time consuming. This binder style lifebook is started as soon as the decision is made to accept the child into our home and includes the notes from the initial phone conversation from the placement worker Laurie, which starts it all off. I also add in accurate notes from meetings and court case hearings.

Within the first few days of the child being placed in our home, a family team meeting will be set up. This is an important meeting that includes the agency staff, the child's parents/family, and the foster parents (usually). The purpose is to gather pertinent information about the child. After the meeting is completed, I ask to take a family picture for the child's lifebook. I explain briefly to the child's family what a lifebook is, why we make one, and that a family photo would be a meaningful page if they are agreeable. I have never been refused permission to take the photo and have been told on more than one occasion that this is the first time a full family picture has ever been taken.

One mom's answer to my picture request was that she would take a photo but that the father of her child had never allowed pictures of himself to be taken. Surprisingly, the dad looked at me, nodded slightly, and agreed to one photo. He is now incarcerated for life, and this is the one photo the child has of herself with both of her parents together. In another instance, the mom of our foster baby overdosed and died a few weeks after the family team meeting. After a while, I contacted the baby's grieving grandmother to express our condolences and inform her that I had several beautiful pictures of her daughter and granddaughter together from this family team meeting a month earlier. The family was overwhelmed with gratitude for the beautiful photos. Advocating for the child by getting a family photo is a profoundly important piece of history and a special gift we can give them.

I let our foster child's family know that I will give their children an extra copy of the family photo to keep for themselves too. A few photos of the children's family displayed in our home shows a good faith effort to make the house feel a bit like the child's too. For small children, we place a laminated copy of the cherished family photo on the refrigerator for them to tug off and carry around with as they please. We laminate the photo to preserve them from sticky fingers and drooling mouths. Little ones absolutely love this sentiment and play with the photos every day. It is so cute when one tot finds another tot's photo on the floor and waddles over to give it to me to replace on the refrigerator. They can show some incredible empathy even at a young age.

As days, weeks, months, and sometimes years go on, we include photos of special outings in the child's lifebook. Photos of their own family events or visits are also added if the child's family chooses to provide them. Additionally, medical summary notes from doctor visits, school assessments, and a few arts and crafts pages are added to the lifebook. I also add comments about milestones such as when they roll over or take their first steps. All papers are preserved in the correct order and timeline. Basically, every piece of paper that passes through our home for a foster child is filed in the lifebook, given to the child's case manager or parents, or is trashed. These books help us stay organized. This was definitely necessary when we had eight foster children one winter.

Years ago, we had a set of brothers for whom we made some of our first lifebooks. After the parents' case plan failed, the children left our home and were adopted out of town. We met up with them years later and they told us how much those lifebooks meant to them. They told me they grew up with their lifebooks "always" on their nightstands and their adoptive mom would occasionally add photos too. From then on, we would visit them every year or two, snap a photo to commemorate the day, and send the boys each a copy to add into their lifebooks. They tell us, thirty years later, that they still cherish those lifebooks, and we assure them that we still completely cherish them too!

Lifebooks make it fun for children to look back on activities they got to participate in while in foster care, such as sporting events, school plays, or summer camp. Therapists and social workers also like looking through the books at visits with the children because it gives them a glimpse into the day-to-day activities of the child's life and provides prompts for conversation—especially with teens. Excessively shy, withdrawn, or nonverbal children often use the lifebook to connect with these adults. The books help them put the events of their time in foster care into words and allow them to remember their foster family, neighbors, and school friends they often become close to. Since by nature we highlight positive aspects of childhood and downplay negatives, it's a great self-esteem builder too.

On two different occasions we had six foster children placed with us from three different families. The method of lifebook documentation was immensely helpful in keeping the paperwork from medical appointments to coloring papers with the right child from the right family. As sibling groups are getting ready to leave our home, we will make copies of some of the lifebook pages to send with each sibling, especially if they are going to different placements, which unfortunately does happen. If the child's case would eventually progress to permanent custody status, the information in the lifebook will be greatly appreciated by the child's new adoptive family.

Both parents of drug-exposed baby Jessa attended the initial family team meeting shortly after she came to our foster home. After the paperwork for the family's medical history and case-plan objectives were completed, the parents left the family team meeting and never returned. The notes and family photo from this meeting were literally the bulk of the information the adoptive family got from us for this little one when she was adopted. The lifebook might not have been as in depth as we would have liked, but they were very grateful to have every word of information in it.

We survived two action-packed years with four young siblings in our care. Because there was so much information collected in the time the children spent in our home, it led to four fully filled 3" lifebook volumes. Years later, a lead blood test result was needed for one of the children, and the family was able to find the result in the lifebook documentation. They called to thank me because the elevated lead level information qualified them for the removal of lead-based paint from their basement through a community grant. For the foster children's family, the lifebook serves as an accurate record of the child's life in foster care and is an important layer of love that you are sending each child home wrapped in.

All children cherish memory books, and we parents feel we did a good job taking the time to document their lives. I made scrapbooks for our own children of the highlights of their lives up through and including high school graduation, so I think this is a great tool for any family to use. Accentuating the positive moments of a child's upbringing is the goal. We have many darling video clips of children's reactions as they meander through their lifebooks reminiscing over memories.

Ron and I complete each lifebook with a personalized "graduation from foster care" letter. This heartfelt sentiment is written to the children as we wish them well on the next leg of their personal journey. We tell them how much they meant to us and that they will be remembered, loved, and prayed for forever. That last page is usually filled with tears and kisses. After that closing letter, the book and child are ready to be sent along. Grief is the price we pay for love. Surely the children know what we mean when we say, once you are in a foster parent's heart, you never fully leave.

MAGIC BOXES

Magic boxes store memories that are too big to put in children's lifebooks and are too cherished to discard. We use plastic storage bins for children to keep their treasures in. While we try to take pictures of as many beloved crafts, art activities, and school projects as we can so we can discard the actual projects and keep just the photo, all children have some beloved items they want to keep. Magic boxes are "magic" because they help us travel back through time to relive a treasured memory.

Karen was a pack rat and had such anxiety when it came to thinning out any of her material possessions. She ended up collecting three full magic boxes filled with her endless scraps of paper and every paperclip she ever touched, instead of one bin that all her brothers and sisters managed to get by with. While we had the best intentions to keep a reasonable amount of memorabilia for Karen, she had other plans. What worked for four of the five children did not work for her. Understanding the need to personalize care for a child is definitely at the heart of what active parents believe.

IN CLOSING

Parents work hard! The behaviors we see from our children can be challenging. No one makes it through parenting completely unscathed. In addition, facing the modern challenges of blended families means we need to depend on each other for valuable support and advice. Sadly, we are seeing consequences in our society because of ineffective, inactive parenting.

Strong families and communities support parents. I believe households that have extra time to spare can be of value to ones struggling. The value of a family and generational help cannot be overstated. I am unapologetically a fan of the TV series *The Waltons*. They understood how generations of families living near or with each other create a priceless support system.

Grandparents as well as present fathers being active are huge factors in stability for the child. I know many single parent families who are doing a great job with their children, but I also see a pattern with them where they have found an uncle, cousin, or grandparent who helps fill in the role of the missing parent. An epidemic of unstable homes is making many families seem disposable. We need to get back to some form of the whole family support system to make a more stable society.

Caring people wanting others to succeed adds strength to our vulnerable families and sometimes shaky society. Protecting children from suffering trauma in the first place should be the initial focus. Then secondary would be the need to help each other heal from trauma that has already occurred, by being a better support to each other. The best chance of surviving parenting is to work diligently to learn to be an active parent, swap clever ideas with each other, and form iron-strong support networks.

While meeting all the children's needs during the time they are in our care, whatever the circumstance, is not possible, they *will* remember the way they were helped to begin to conquer their problems and learn to cope with future stresses. They *will* remember the kind attention given to them. They *will* remember the learned coping skills helping them understand what trauma is and how to grow through it. Their emotional intelligence *will* grow, and their emotional bonding *will* be more secure. They *will* know that life might not be perfect, but it is still good!

Once we train ourselves in these techniques, we are better at curbing their negative antics and can see the children's true personalities bloom. Still, at times, all parenting techniques fall short. We do not have an answer to every situation. We are all trying to find ingenious and agreeable solutions to problems that arise. Every well-thought-out choice is a step in building a hope-filled, confident child who has a strong foundation. So, in whatever way you are parenting, reach out for help. Try your best, do not expect a concrete endings to problems, and find joy in the moments, otherwise you will feel like life is passing you by as you wait for that perfect day.

Our focus is to keep children safe, create ones who are socially strong and morally just, and help them all grow into their full potential. We can only do this with patience, active parenting skills, and never-ending love. The key is that we do not feel the need to dwell endlessly on bad moments or bad days. They will pass and the situation will change in some way by the next day. We pray for strength to cheerfully give more of ourselves as parents than we think is possible.

We should all use our God-given talents to protect and heal children, never take advantage of them, and help them find their momentum in life. Let's cheerfully and lovingly guide them toward better behaviors so they can flourish. Then we will witness more stable youth and teens who grow into well-adjusted adults and who can raise the next generation with stability too. Most importantly, we aim to reflect God back to others. When we look in the mirror at night, we want to like who we see.

EPILOGUE

We remember to laugh and enjoy our foster children and their families. We have been privileged to experience so many funny moments in our foster-care career. Having fond memories helps balance out the really tough days. Here are a few favorite memories and sayings that bring such joy to reminisce over.

Small children and unusual names go hand in hand. Our foster children have labeled us with several nicknames. Ron ends up with typical titles like Mr. Ron, Misser On ("Rs" are a challenge for the littles), and Foster Dad. He had to stop the "Yo Bruh" title one day recently, even though he was chuckling underneath. I have been called Sasseen, Caffeine, Kabaleen, and best of all Mr. Mommy because LaShay said, "It just goes better with Mr. Ron." Even today, over a decade later, she still calls me Mr. Mommy.

We chuckle at the funny things the children say. Libby did not want a snack near her while she was doing homework, or she would get too "astracted." Gabby as a young toddler said, "Okay, Mom, okay" with the appropriate two-year-old eye roll whenever a request was made of her precious time. Bruce pointed to the "heppicopters" up in the sky, and Noah always wanted a turn holding the "commote retrol." Yasie walked in and stated in an incredulous voice, "You have two bathrooms. That's amazing!" Katie thought every princess movie was "atastic!" Jabril said to listen carefully to the teacher and her "constructions." Clyde carried around a giant stuffed black bear the entire year he lived here and called it "dada." Tyreke answered my "How was your day?" questions with "ish" and a big toothy grin. Moanna's mom called her baby daughter "Mama," so every time a call went out in my house for mama, both she and I answered simultaneously. Lastly, Louisa told us on the day she left that she "really liked" us, after telling us for a year that she didn't.

We constantly recall all the darling moments that make the days of parenting worthwhile. Aisha loved to put "Chaslix" on her dry lips at night. Simone always said "look ahind you Mommy look ahind you!" Baby Cedrik had the cutest little pout that got him dubbed "grumpy baby," which then made him laugh when we called him that. Zain at fourteen months old stomped around with a big attitude and a husky swagger all his own, so he was known as our little Tonka truck. Eight-month-old Steph would lean her head into her eighteen-month-old brother's face signaling that she needed a kiss from him.

Many songs and movies make us think of certain children too. Aleigha sang "Elmo's World" practically nonstop and counted out loud every step she ever climbed. Tianna sang "Let It Go" at the top of her little voice because I think she related to the sisters losing their mother and father and being orphans. Tre's favorite holiday song as a little one was "Jingle Bells," and his toothless words went something like this: "Jingle belllths, jingle belllths, jingle all the way, Oh McFun it is to ride . . . "

Yasie told me one day that she liked all our special nicknames that we call her like sweetie pie and cutie, but "I like sunsign [her version of sunshine] the best!" One day, little two-year-old Bridget was holding her stomach as she threw up on the brand-new carpet in her room. When I ran in to help, I said, "My carpet!" After that, whenever she got a stomachache, she grabbed her stomach and said, "My carpet hurts." Geez, mom of the year award for that one!

Maybe one of my favorite memorable takeaways from children is the pictures they draw or color. I cherish the various drawings from dozens of foster children's renditions of what our family looked like that day. The pictures still hang on our kitchen cupboards. I adore looking at the carefully crafted works of art because they are our family's history. It is ironic because no two pictures have the exact same family members in it. It is a privilege to think back to each special child and the specific time they lived here with us.

"I feel that we too often focus on the negative aspects of life, on what is bad. If we were more willing to see the good and the beautiful things that surround us, we would be able to transform society. It begins in the family. From there, we can help transform our next-door neighbors with loving service, then others who live in our neighborhood and city. We can bring peace and love to the world. The whole world is hungry for these things, and we can each play a small role in feeding this great hunger."[12] – *St. Teresa of Calcutta*

END NOTES

1. Centers for Disease Control and Prevention, "Fast Facts: Preventing Adverse Childhood Experiences," June 29, 2023, cdc.gov/violenceprevention/aces/fastfact.html.

2. National Child Traumatic Stress Network, "Complex Trauma," Accessed April 19, 2024, nctsn.org/what-is-child-trauma/trauma-types/complex-trauma.

3. Bremner, J.D., "Traumatic Stress: Effects on the Brain," *Dialogues in Clinical Neuroscience*, 2006 Dec; 8(4): 445–461. ncbi.nlm.nih.gov/pmc/articles/PMC3181836.

4. Ibid.

5. Cline, F., & Fay, J. *Parenting with Love & Logic: Teaching Children Responsibility.* (2020). NavPress.

6. Rees, C., "Childhood Attachment," *The British Journal of General Practice*: Nov 1; 57(544): 920–922,

ncbi.nlm.nih.gov/pmc/articles/PMC2169321.

7. Rollè, L., et al., "Father Involvement and Cognitive Development in Early and Middle Childhood: A Systematic Review," *Frontiers in Psychology*, October 24, 2019, frontiersin.org/articles/10.3389/fpsyg.2019.02405/full.

8. Kendra Cherry, MSEd, "How to Prevent Brain Shrinkage with Age," Verywell Mind, January 29, 2024, verywellmind.com/prevent-brain-shrinkage-2795016.

9. Lockett, E., "Can Excessive Screen Time Cause 'Digital Dementia'?" Healthline, February 2, 2024, healthline.com/health/parenting/digital-dementia#prevention.

10. Mother Teresa and Matthew Kelley. *Do Something Beautiful for God: The Essential Teachings of Mother Teresa.* November 15, 2019. Blue Sparrow.

11. *The AFCARS Report*, The U.S. Department of Health and Human Services, Administration for Children and Families, Administration on Children, Youth and Families, Children's Bureau, June 28, 2022, acf.hhs.gov/sites/default/files/documents/cb/afcars-report-29.pdf.

12. Mother Teresa and Matthew Kelley. *Do Something Beautiful for God: The Essential Teachings of Mother Teresa.* November 15, 2019. Blue Sparrow.

ABOUT THE AUTHOR

Kathleen and her husband, Ron, reside in Wadsworth, Ohio. They love spending time with their adult children and participating in the events in their lives.

Kathleen's favorite memories happen around her front porch while catching up with family and friends. She loves to garden and teach children to plant, and at harvest time she delights in small pleasures like watching strawberry juice trickle down the faces of their smiling children. She also treasures the time spent woodworking with her dad. Kathleen and Ron advocate for children in the foster-care system through appearances and speaking engagements.

Kathleen has also authored the book *Fostering Love: A Glimpse into Foster Care*, which chronicles real-life stories of the devastation that abuse and neglect cause and how children in foster care have taught us the immense impact— good and bad—that parents have on them. When we care for and protect children, we ensure that future generations thrive as well. Learn more at kathleenpaydo.com.

www.ingramcontent.com/pod-product-compliance
Lightning Source LLC
Chambersburg PA
CBHW051301120626
46547CB00015B/2037